AIJA LULLE

MIDLIFE GEOGRAPHIES

Changing Lifecourses across Generations, Spaces and Time

First published in Great Britain in 2024 by

Bristol University Press
University of Bristol
1–9 Old Park Hill
Bristol
BS2 8BB
UK
t: +44 (0)117 374 6645
e: bup-info@bristol.ac.uk

Details of international sales and distribution partners are available at
bristoluniversitypress.co.uk

© Bristol University Press 2024

British Library Cataloguing in Publication Data
A catalogue record for this book is available from the British Library

ISBN 978-1-5292-2887-8 hardcover
ISBN 978-1-5292-2888-5 ePub
ISBN 978-1-5292-2889-2 ePdf

The right of Aija Lulle to be identified as author of this work has been asserted by her in accordance with the Copyright, Designs and Patents Act 1988.

All rights reserved: no part of this publication may be reproduced, stored in a retrieval system, or transmitted in any form or by any means, electronic, mechanical, photocopying, recording, or otherwise without the prior permission of Bristol University Press.

Every reasonable effort has been made to obtain permission to reproduce copyrighted material. If, however, anyone knows of an oversight, please contact the publisher.

The statements and opinions contained within this publication are solely those of the author and not of the University of Bristol or Bristol University Press. The University of Bristol and Bristol University Press disclaim responsibility for any injury to persons or property resulting from any material published in this publication.

Bristol University Press works to counter discrimination on grounds of gender, race, disability, age and sexuality.

Cover design: Blu Inc
Front cover image: 'Emily' by Sari Soininen
Bristol University Press uses environmentally responsible print partners.
Printed and bound in Great Britain by CPI Group (UK) Ltd, Croydon, CR0 4YY

Contents

Acknowledgements iv

one	Introduction: Midlife	1
two	Ways of Talking about Midlife	18
three	Midlife Transitions: Body and Work	30
four	Midlife Transitions: Home and Relationships	59
five	Geographies of Menopausing	77
six	Conclusions: Policy Focus	99

References 111
Index 131

Acknowledgements

Thank you, Sari Soininen, for your permission to use your fabulous art photo as the cover for this book! I am grateful to Anna Richardson and Emily Watt (Bristol University Press) for their patience and helpful guidance. Daniel Edward Allen and Maggie Reid, thank you for language editing. Many thanks go to Liene Čīma, Ieva Morica, Ute Karl, Laura Moroşanu, Linda Lapiņa, Pauliina Lukinmaa, Zaina Gadema, Tanja Bastia, Elham Amini and Klāvs Sedlenieks for sharing great ideas and your work, or reading parts of the manuscript. I am grateful to Megha Amrith, Dora Sampaio, Victoria Shakti and Swetlana Torno for wonderful conversations during my visit to the Max Planck Institute in 2023. I benefited from discussions at the IMISCOE conference in Warsaw in 2023, where Dora and I organized a panel on middle-aged migrants. My thanks go to my dear Loughborough University colleagues Sarah Holloway, Sophie Cranston, Marco Antonsich and others who commented on very early ideas for this book in 2021. I received funding from the (Re)moving Ties: Relatedness in Contemporary Mobile Work Regimes project (lzp-2021/1-0213), funded by the Latvian Council of Science, and from the University of Eastern Finland for my Returning Home? Making and Imagining Ageing Futures project.

ONE

Introduction: Midlife

Introduction

I could not write for a year. For the first time since I can remember in my writing career, I literally could not type anything more than short sentences. Consequently, I postponed submission of this book. In hindsight, I believe that might have been a blessing in disguise. Prior to this pause in my writing, my intention was to create a book that could serve as a primer on geographical approaches to midlife in the context of our rapidly ageing world in the 21st century. I wanted to explore questions such as: What is midlife? How is it changing? Answers to these questions, which are bound by lifecourse, time and space, are long overdue in geography. I observed a dearth of research on midlife geographies, in stark contrast to the extensive studies on geographies of children, youth and older age over the past decade. As part of the 'sandwich' generation, individuals in midlife bear the heavy burden of both work and caregiving. Nevertheless, this crucial and shifting middle-aged cohort has received inadequate attention in the realms of geographical and social sciences scholarship.

However, both my life and the way I approached writing this book underwent significant changes. Instead of engaging in writing, I delved into extensive reading. Furthermore, I immersed myself in fieldwork, researching ageing in one project and studying transnational families and mobile individuals in another. This shift allowed me to discover the art of listening and observing with fresh eyes (Rubin and

Rubin 2005). On revisiting interviews and field diaries from my earlier research on youth and ageing, I noticed elements that had previously eluded my understanding. These pertained to midlife as a significant process with its turning points, repertoires borrowed from popular media, reflections on life and relationships, and bodily changes. I realized that my personal experiences since completing those studies – with major turning points in my working life, the death of my father, ageing relatives and the challenges of raising a child transnationally, plus the sudden onset of anxiety and health scare – meant that I was a different researcher now compared to 10 or 15 years ago.

I was born in Latvia in the mid-1970s. After university, I worked as a journalist, and later, during 2010–2014, I pursued my PhD as a 'mature' student, studying middle-aged and ageing migrants from Latvia. As an early career researcher, I grasped what I could theoretically and through observation from my own vantage points. While not inherently superior or inferior to my current lifecourse positionality, those vantage points were undeniably different. Lived experience holds value – this realization has grown ever stronger for me in the past couple of years. My positionality and gendered, embodied experience matter significantly, especially in the context of midlife, where many narratives are accessible to the middle generation but not understood by younger or even older generations. Rather than creating a more representative and, perhaps, drier primer on midlife geographies, I decided that it was crucial to incorporate my positionality and draw on the field notes from my research. While this approach inevitably means the book is more subjective, it does not necessarily compromise rigor.

Things took an unexpected turn for me when I experienced poor health. I do not want to bore you with my 'symptomology', but the short string of events went like this. In mid-2022 I got a temporary job in Finland, where my family lives. I left my stable job at Loughborough University in the UK – where I had worked, in my mid-forties, during 2018–2022 – in a rush, but fell ill with COVID-19. Then, when I reached Finland, I fell ill with Lyme disease. I could not sleep and was physically and mentally unwell. Having been healthy all my life, I was completely unprepared for the myriad symptoms I experienced, from high anxiety to bodily pain. In the midst of exhaustion, and even with debilitating shoulder pain, I did manage some tasks. 'You are in pain', a fellow researcher a couple of years my senior remarked. Later on, I told her that I was working on a book about midlife geographies. 'But how can you write about what you have not experienced?' she wondered. It took me several excruciating months to connect the dots. Then, on top of the coronavirus and bacterial infection, let alone all the tribulations of our times that were about to unfold, I entered perimenopause – something I was not prepared for. My (well-founded) health fears were not taken seriously, and I realized that an early midlife can be a dangerous time and space for a migrant woman like me. It was in Lock's (1993) and Amini's (2023) books that I found some answers about menopausing and narratives of ill-being. I also underestimated how challenging the move from a stable job to fixed-term employment would be for my professional identity in midlife. I began radically rethinking whose knowledge on midlife counts and how I wanted this short book to unfold (cf Harding 1991).

My experience as a researcher and middle-aged migrant woman are unapologetically important. They matter for my awareness of vulnerability, shame and fear, all concepts that my research on midlife, and specifically menopause geographies, tackles. I admit my not-so-conscious influences from neoliberal culture, which feed into my striving to be a strong high achiever and someone who takes matters of my wellbeing into my own hands. Fighting anxiety and tiredness – and thinking these symptoms were related to having both a teenager and a cancer survivor in a transnational home – I ordered the health supplement gamma-aminobutyric acid (GABA) from one of the most popular supplement websites, iHerb. However, Finnish customs officials, without informing me, launched an investigation against me for bringing a forbidden substance onto Finnish territory. I was shocked and felt betrayed, as my intention when buying GABA was only to be able to care better for others and myself. The case was abandoned because, as a custom's officer later reported, the amount was very small and, in any case, it is possible to buy GABA in some Finnish supplement shops. A couple of years later, Finnish authorities made an official announcement prohibiting the import of several popular health supplements available via the iHerb site. This experience led me to fine-tune my attention to the relationship between midlife and the networked market of health supplements, which I discuss in Chapter 3.

When I worked at Loughborough University, female professors openly spoke about menopause and made changes to the environment to improve the workplace for all. When I travelled back home to Finland and to visit Latvia, I would share the empowerment I felt in my British workplace, but such open discussions on menopausing were uncomfortable for some of my acquaintances in Finland and Latvia. Even in various medical practitioners' offices, when I mentioned hormonal changes, I was met with untranslatable silence and lack of response. Since entering my late forties, I have visited gynaecologists in two countries to observe how different scientific knowledge of menopause timing is communicated and how unequal the supply chains of prescription hormone treatment are. The language that doctors used on these occasions, which I also started noticing more often in popular writing and podcasts, was that of a schizophrenic division of the body. 'Your ovaries are getting lazy', I was once told. This stung me as a migration researcher and a migrant woman, given the ubiquitous accusation that migrants are lazy and unfit to produce for local wealth. However, it also made me laugh as I cannot command my ovaries, through willpower or neoliberal techniques, to be more enthusiastic. At the same time, it made me feel sad. Is this how women talk about their own bodies and play into denigrating discourses of patriarchy and ageism? In Chapter 2, I show how people talk about midlife bodies, but I also push beyond any misery and demonstrate that more hopeful, creative and dignified ways to narrate midlife are available in the public sphere.

Having paid hefty amounts of money to access healthcare, as female health is not included in my work medical insurance in Finland, I realized the financial inequality this entails for middle-aged people. Traumatized by the GABA incident, I often searched with a certain amount of trepidation for information on whether I could carry melatonin, bought over the counter in Finland, when I travelled to other countries, as it is age restricted in the UK and not licenced in Sweden. I joined digital spaces with women discussing menopause and saw that my terrible experiences were far from an exception. On the contrary, these experiences highlighted the relevance of the geography of menopause in ways I could not imagine reading in the medical literature. In the meantime, as I was writing the book, Finland was introducing educative debates by doctors and public figures on the topic of female health. Around this time, Heinonen's (2021) book suggested GABA as a functional medicine support for menopause 'problems'. Here was a turning point in my thinking, and I decided to write both subjectively and more actively. My experience and awareness that, like many, I am vulnerable to marketing aimed at middle-aged consumers (usually the best payers) made me acutely attentive to how capitalism cashes in on people who seek to live better lives, while philosophies on how to produce more adequate work and rest spaces and times lag behind (Del Casino 2009).

To sum up, throughout the book, I draw on insights from various sources, including my own autoethnographic vignettes and field notes (see Duncan 2004). In seeking relations between generations, diverse lifecourses and genders, I methodologically quilt (Saukko 2000), or stitch together, philosophies and research traditions that cannot be comfortably subsumed under one framework. However, the guiding principles of this book do offer a direction and a pattern for my proposed patchwork. I seek to uncover lived experience, rather than producing a generalized reductionism of what midlife is. Moreover, gendered geographies of power equip me with praxis-oriented analysis (Mahler and Pessar 2001), and instead of accepting that midlife is poorly understood and overlooked, I seek to propose ideas for what people can do, focusing on social transformation and emancipation as well as nurturing a hope for a world where people in middle age can live more fulfilling lives.

Theoretical departure points

The aim of this book is to create knowledge on the diverse relationships between time, space and people in midlife. There is a cohort of middle-aged people who matured through the turbulent 1980s and 1990s, which saw a massive shift towards neoliberalism, and still have important decades of their productive lives ahead. The book, therefore, critically questions how people's lives actually transform after youth and before older age.

Life transition theories usually start like fairy tales: young people transition (however bumpy and unconventional such transitions can be) from school to work to stable jobs, a family and their own home. But here the theory (and the fairy tale) usually ends (Arnett 2001). Later in life, people experience ageing transitions that begin around the time they start thinking about retirement, or when they are already are retired, broadly speaking (Lulle 2019; 2021). The middle part of life remains opaque and unexplained. Well, there are no shortages of demographic or psychological approaches, but the sense remains that something akin to a fault-line exists between youth and older age. This book looks directly at this so far rather poorly explained middle part of the lifecourse.

INTRODUCTION

The book unpacks two related arguments. First, I look at midlife as a relational phenomenon with its own temporalities and spatialities. Through the lens of midlife, we can trace connections to and separations from other major lifecourse categories. I argue that midlife is produced politically, socioculturally and economically through intergenerational relations and demands that are both placed on individuals and self-imposed. Second, midlife geographies today must be viewed against the horizons of population change and the global neoliberal shift (Bastia et al 2022). Populations around the world, and in the Global North in particular, are ageing rapidly (United Nations Department of Economic and Social Affairs 2019). However, before the world gets old, it will be home to large cohorts of people in midlife. Extraordinary population changes will force governments to not only compete for younger migrants (Vollset et al 2020) but also, more fundamentally, recognize that the mid-lifecourse is changing. It is, therefore, paradoxical that this period of high-level activity in midlife is only sporadically explored in human geography or, as Hopkins and Pain (2007: 288) put it, midlife geographies 'are missing all together'. The understanding of when people are in midlife is changing rapidly and in spatially diversified ways. In the chapters of this book, I lay out ways in which we understand mid-lifecourse today.

Therefore, midlife serves as a lens through which we can expose, in a timely way, the workings and instability of fundamental categories in the social sciences: neoliberal capitalism; class; and inclusion and exclusion in institutions such as the family, the state, education and the labour market. I also argue for close attention to the body scale in midlife, because people live their lives and make sense of the world through their bodies in the particular places where they live. Also, lifecourse research on midlife typically focuses on care and relationships (Moen 2003; Lachman 2001; Stockdale et al 2013). I build on the geographical lifecourse approach of linked lives (Findlay et al 2015) and explore transnational social fields, filled with histories and ongoing relationships.

The main aim here is to demonstrate how we can explore the mid-lifecourse in more diverse ways and illuminate the centrality of sociospatiality and temporality in people's lives. I base my understanding of lifecourses as ever-evolving multiple social time-spaces (May and Thrift 2001; Massey 2005). It is through the logic of intra- and intergenerational relations that we see best how broader processes of inequality play out and how social difference works dynamically, and zooming in on the shifting notions and lived experiences of midlife can reveal these larger processes in a new light. Therefore, this book is guided by intersectional feminism (Crenshaw 1991) and feminist geographical imagination. These approaches urge us to examine 'our' and 'other' spaces through the lens of difference and through concrete embodied experiences (Bastia 2019; Rose 1993). Feminist ethics argues for uncovering the standpoints of those who are overlooked; it claims that the personal is political, and there is certainly a politics of midlife which must be brought into focus in research. The intersectional perspective proposes an understanding of how social differences – gender, age, class, ethnicity and other differences – shape life opportunities. I further sensitize this approach to time and space dynamics, which create differentiated opportunities and limitations for people in their middle age.

I therefore direct theoretical attention towards novel ways of understanding midlife times and spaces, moving beyond the unreflective packaging of people in age categories. I make contributions to existing theories which run short by describing midlife in terms of limited realms of care and personal relationships. Care does not exist apart from work; care is work and caring duties fundamentally shape paid work, especially in individualistic neoliberal frameworks. Care in midlife can be 'forced' instead of being an option for those who care. Conversely, care as a lifestyle in middle age can be a privilege which few can afford. Simultaneously, lifestyle or class aspirations do not exist independently of lifecourse; people create their lifestyle intersectionally, relationally and through geographic arbitrage. I argue that midlife is differentiated spatially and over time, because space and mobilities are always imbued with politics and intergenerational time (Giddens 1991). More so, the ways in which work spaces and work times are created in the capitalist world should be scrutinized through lived experiences of diversity, which reveal that these orders are oppressive and inconsiderate for people with diverse responsibilities, needs and bodily changes in midlife.

I have delved into dominant demographic approaches to midlife, scrutinizing how it has been conceptualized and exploring the interests of demographers and geographers who employ demographic methods. I found that these approaches often generalize lifecourses too broadly, obscuring the real lives behind the data. For example, stating that most people are at their prime income and health during midlife (as was the case with the MIDUS – Midlife in the United States – study in the US context, carried out between 1995 and 2013; see MIDUS nd) can hide more than it reveals, especially for those facing precarious labour markets and racial and gender disparities, and when it comes to human relationships with places. This realization prompted me to seek research on how lifecourses unfold across different geographical contexts, particularly through the lens of gendered geographies, which turned out to be diverse but fragmented. I began to identify patterns of social and economic transitions and processes shaped by cultural ideas of midlife and ageing. My ongoing interest in migration led me to explore not only the experiences of those who move but also their relationships and transnational networks. Midlife is arguably the most important vantage point through which we can see how distinctions between the migrant and the expat are lived out. In addition, despite the challenges that middle-aged mobile people face everywhere due to their embedded networks and care duties in different places, social differences show us how structures play a crucial role in amplifying or reducing life chances in midlife and how they shape people's ageing futures.

While social research provided valuable insights, I felt a sense of lack in discussions about midlife, and this prompted me to turn to popular literature and the humanities. Popular literature offers sharply gendered perspectives and depicts dramas that might seem trivial to social researchers emphasizing self-defined rigor and replicability of data. The humanities, with its attention to geographical contexts, enriches our understanding of where midlife unfolds, from demographic shifts to intimate homes. In the chapters that follow, I explore what geographers can learn from the humanities literature. Additionally, my exploration of books on midlife challenged and reshaped my understanding of how masculine philosophical and psychological texts muse on midlife – a topic I delve into in Chapter 2.

Youth transitions data reminded me of how culturally despised adulthood, especially midlife, can be among young people. Adulthood can be dreaded as it is seen as boring, exhausting, futureless (Lulle et al 2022). In the widely popularized neoliberal culture of achievement, perpetual growth, individualism and choice, this period of life is seen as an inevitable clash of all these fairy tales. When young adults feel trapped in long hours working and commuting, and the rat race of promotions, they feel old. Many of them delay having children as this is a definite sign that youth is over, and they see the burdens of everyday life as preventing them from having everything that neoliberal youth culture presents as valuable. The extensive geographical research on youth, the lack of studies on midlife and the geographies of ageing that portray older age as inevitably involving constrained times and spaces play along with this dominant culture of youth, despite the fact that demographic ageing reality suggests otherwise in many societies today. People do not want to be seen as 'old'. This is not their denial of the ageing process as such; rather, it is their resistance to massive and ubiquitous structural barriers that prevent them from living their lives to the full. Ageism marginalizes, labels and excludes.

Methodological considerations

As a geographer, and a migration scholar in particular, I look at both migrants and non-migrants to uncover the layers of midlife experience for people who stay put and those who are on the move. Most of the empirical examples in the book are from the three, rather different, countries that I know best and where I have carried out research: the UK, a capitalist economy of a global scale; Finland, a Nordic welfare state; and Latvia, which embarked on a neoliberal economic path in the early 1990s.

I use data from my research in Latvia, Finland and the UK during 2018–2020, when I interviewed return and transnational migrants as well as those who never migrated, which then later morphed into my Returning Home? Making and Imagining Ageing Futures project, funded by the University of Eastern Finland (2022–2023). These data provide insights into geographies of home in midlife, how migration shapes home practices socially and economically, and the differences that urban and rural dwellings or moves between these settings make. The data, based on interviews and considerable time spent with people to see how they produce space, provide a broad range of observations on how the body lives in midlife, what the health considerations are, and how issues of care, inheritance and many other midlife considerations play out in everyday life. Some of the research participants who were in their sixties, in good health and recently retired or semi-retired saw themselves as living the best part of their midlife rather than being 'young-old'. These individuals were freer of the clutches of daily grinding paid jobs than they had been in their younger adult years, and often they were free from hands-on care. They were active and happy in the care, cultural and travel choices they made.

Hence, the fairy tale of a neoliberal winner and chooser shone its light somewhere around retirement for these people, who were healthy and did not have pressing financial circumstances.

I also draw on insights from the Removing Ties: Relatedness in Contemporary Mobile Work Regimes project, funded by the Latvian Council of Science and Rīga Stradiņš University (2022–2024). As part of this project, I interviewed academics, diplomats and other highly skilled professionals whose job requires them to move between countries more or less regularly. Most were in midlife, and the interviews covered young midlife to changes in one's fifties and entering into early retirement. Their specific work-related arrangements allow me to illuminate the role of privilege and protection. In addition, their status of being highly skilled and earning relatively helps me consider the role of class and social status in shaping midlife experiences of body changes and work, and how preparations for retirement differ for those who have worked in jobs that are lower-paid and less protected.

In the realm of secondary sources, I refer to findings from several large-scale surveys exploring how people navigate midlife, mainly within the US context, utilizing data collected a decade and two decades ago. Given my personal connection to the former Soviet Union, I also consider data on transitions from youth to midlife in post-socialist contexts.

Overview of chapters

Through extensive reading, I realized that the academic studies on midlife, menopause and similar significant concepts which claim representativeness may fall short due to the shaky foundational ideas on which they are built. Apart from this, the majority of discussions about midlife actually do not happen in academic ivory towers, but take place in the media and in the multimillion-dollar industry of novels, self-help books and guides targeting people in midlife. Midlife themes are also incredibly popular in digital spaces and blogs, where

INTRODUCTION

people tell their stories while finding refuge in anonymity and, at the same time, some sense of belonging and similarity with others. I therefore begin Chapter 2 not with a theory of lifecourse per se, but by describing these ways of producing spaces where narratives of midlife are crafted. In addition, as I completed this book, a new wave of menopause activism was emerging. Hence, quite a large part of the book is devoted to a long-overdue look at menopause geographies, which I claim must be taken seriously in the agendas of social and cultural geographers, and beyond. I draw on data on midlife from various social research sources and incorporate references from medical and popular literature recognizing menopause as a vital but often overlooked process in midlife geographies.

Chapter 2 is, therefore, about narratives. A narrative approach is crucial to break silences and confront taken-for-granted stereotypes and ageist tropes about middle-aged people, which, inadvertently or unreflexively, can also inform social research. I look at several narrative strands that are shaping ways of talking about midlife and may increase people's capacity to re-self and make substantial shifts in how they narrate themselves (Goodson et al 2012: 8). I begin with a review of psychological and philosophical texts from the male perspective, analysing how these depict this life stage and what processes they silence. The analysis then moves to the feminist narration on midlife. Here, I apply a reparatory lens to the long-entrenched proposition of misery as a motif of the female encounter with ageing in midlife. I also analyse several written texts and television programmes from various genres I have engaged with, seeking to decipher these with a more emancipatory agenda in mind. Through analysis of these texts and television programmes, I interpret cultural representations from Latvian, Finnish and British contexts (cf Geertz 1973; Gupta and Ferguson 1997).

In chapters 3 and 4, I analyse how midlife mobilities differ from the social and geographical transitions in youth and older age. I also examine how midlife mobilities are experienced in work, lifestyle and (im)mobility, how people in middle age people produce spaces and times, and how structures in workplaces and public spaces, and mobility regimes, enable or constrain lives in middle age. Ultimately, the book – which I propose should be seen primarily as a view through the eyes of the people it is about – is concerned with the politics of midlife.

Chapter 3 considers generations of knowledge creation and approaches to midlife. This chapter is concerned with ideas of lifecourse transitions, generations and broader ways in which science produces ideas about midlife. It unpacks the ways in which lifecourse transitions have been conceptualized as linear and why, despite much literature overthrowing this conceptualization, linear imagination and stasis are so persistent when it comes to midlife. Attention to theories of mid-lifecourse also show, in sharp relief, how bodily ageing is so fundamentally embedded in the concept of midlife that it has impoverished other ways of seeing and conceptualizing lifecourse. I contrast these theoretical ideas with lived experience, where ideas from youth and ageing studies are helpful.

Further, chapters 3 and 4 focus on multidirectional time- and place-making in midlife, deepening the so far generally mentioned but less understood relational nature of generativity in midlife – that is, time when we care for both the young and ageing the most. Chapter 4 dives into how people make spaces and places and produce the temporalities that are contingent to midlife. These lived experiences reveal intergenerational time shifts and dynamic claims for individualization, but are often severely constrained by the demands and priorities of others, be this in the home, at work or in public spaces. I show the multiplicity of linked lives and reveal lifecourses as ever evolving. These experiences are ultimately gendered and classed, and they reveal processes of inequality geographically and within sedentary and mobile contexts. Importantly, I also zoom in on practices of awareness and change, where people seek to resist dominant ideas on how they should create relationships or homes.

Chapter 5 is devoted to menopause. As with preceding chapters, this one is also a result of my reading back and forth across various fields of social science literature and some medical literature, but the crucial departure point here comes from medical humanities and Moore's (2022) landmark research on the invention of the concept of menopause by French male medical doctors during the aftermath of the French Revolution. Drawing on a multitude of sources from both academic and popular traditions, I aim to conceptualize menopause geographies anew, seeing this gendered process in life, inevitable for more than half of the world's population, as a temporary and sociospatial process. Hence, recent popular ideas of 'menopausing' (a term coined by McCall and Potter 2022) as a process are relevant stepping stones moving away from reductionist medical approaches in order to build social and cultural geographies of menopausing and analyse the politics of menopausing with distinct geographies that stretch across many domains, including the economy and the geography of supply chains.

Menopause awareness has expanded rapidly over the past few years. In Europe, the centre of this awareness is the UK, where there is regular media reporting on issues related to menopause. Awareness activists include politicians and media personalities, who use their power positions and media platforms to reach broad audiences with documentaries, podcasts and regular meet-ups. There have been top-selling books on the subject, and campaigning by civil society has led to workplace regulations that accommodate the needs of people experiencing menopause, because evidence is mounting in relation to the impact of menopause on job loss, with 10 per cent of job losses being attributed to menopause (UK Parliament 2023). Popular books and podcasts circulate stories of suicidal thoughts and other distressing outcomes for middle-aged women and their loved ones (McCall and Potter 2022; SkyNews 2023; Newson

2023). The use of hormone treatment has spiked exponentially over the past few years, with a sharp increase of 47 per cent in 2023 (Department of Health and Social Care 2023). In the UK, the rise in hormone treatment for menopause symptoms – usually referred to using the pharmaceutical term 'hormone replacement therapy', commonly shortened to 'HRT' – has been criticized by feminist scholars. For instance, Boston Women's Health Collective (2006) argue that the pharmaceutical term 'HRT' is misleading, because it implies that hormones should be replaced to some standard level that exists in youth. In reality, pharmaceutical producers provide various hormone treatment products. While there are no reliable estimates of the global size of the 'natural' supplement industry targeting menopausal people, the hormone therapy business has reached US$20 billion to date. However, due to shortages of hormone treatment and geographical variation in distribution, people drive considerable distances to swap hormone treatment patches despite the prescriptions being strictly regulated by law and prescribed at individual level.

The UK is also championing debates and policies on societal and academic fronts. Parliament has promised to review education policies, make recommendations for teacher and doctor training, and address menopause in the workplace as a significant equality issue (UK Parliament 2023; People Management UK 2023; the Equality Act 2010). Political parties are campaigning for policies to address menopause issues, and universities have cafe hours where menopause is discussed with male colleagues and intergenerationally. This activism has led to numerous achievements, including the National Health Service certificate, which reduces prescription costs for hormone treatment for everyone in need to less than £20 per year (UK Government 2023). One of the world's leading research universities, University College London, has just launched the first course on menopause education.

Awareness and demand have radiated out beyond the UK. In the US, public figures such as Michelle Obama are speaking out about how women are underserved and let down by the lack of high-quality research and policy on menopause issues and urging societal efforts to improve women's lives. Encouraged by the British example, American and Australian activists have submitted proposals for policy change to politicians. In the meantime, in the Baltic country of Latvia, discussion on many menopause-related topics is still rather silenced and stereotyped, while in Finland, there are debates on menopause and informative podcasts, press articles and books by doctors and public figures in the country (for example, Heinonen 2021; Kajan 2023). Also in Finland, there was a recent comedy play performed in Swedish, and a public TV channel broadcasted a documentary, aimed across generations, and a comedy series on the subject. In practice, the experience of menopause in any of these countries is a 'mixed bag'. For example, in Finland menopause symptoms are usually not recognized in occupational medical insurance. This non-recognition can lead to multiple other issues of poor health and wellbeing, including burnout, which requires extended sick leave. Visits to private gynaecologists are very expensive and exacerbate inequality in the already highly unequal access to healthcare for women – particularly migrants and those who are unemployed (Amnesty International 2023). On the other hand, Finnish social services offer discounts of up to 40 per cent on a list of oestrogen products, making treatment more affordable than in the economically worse-off Latvia. In Finland, due to the activism of the Finnish Gynecological Association, menopause has for the first time been mentioned as an occupational health issue in a government policy vision (Suomi 2023).

Finally, in Chapter 6 I summarize the main findings on the knowledge creation of midlife and the ways extant epistemes produce certain views about the lifecourses, spaces and times that middle-aged people inhabit. The chapter is devoted to how these ways of thinking and seeing midlife translate into politics. Under scrutiny are policy agendas on work-life balance, work-life policies and menopause in the workplace.

TWO

Ways of Talking about Midlife

Introduction

The ways people tell stories about midlife are important. With stories, we learn broad contexts, we see what tropes and ideas are perpetuated, abandoned, contested and sometimes resurrected. Some such tropes – for example, 'midlife crisis' (Jaques 1965) – are embraced at certain times and in certain genres, while at other times they are vehemently criticized as an empty invention. At the same time, psychologists argue that midlife, especially gendered midlife, is a pivotal time with complex and changing psychosocial needs (Sherman 1987; Rosenfeld 2004). While the narratives in this chapter are not exhaustive, they crucially shaped the ways in which the people I met and observed as part of my research sought or imagined ways of sailing through midlife.

I look at co-existent perspectives, and narratives and counternarratives, drawing on work by Gullette (2016), who has demonstrated how the overwhelming socialization of the Western cult of youth gave rise to anxieties and neuroses about any signs of ageing. I draw on Frank's (1995) theory from crip studies, productively applied by Amini and McCormack (2019), who have studied menopause in non-Western contexts to discern what kind of storylines about midlife are solidifying in different geographic and social locations. Frank (1995) distinguished between three typical storylines of the wounded storyteller. In Frank's (1995) theory, a chaos story depicts transformations that seem never-ending, while restitution narratives rest on the idea that a normal life and full health can be restored after an unsettling event. In parallel, quest narratives seek transformation, with the protagonist becoming someone new as a result of the experience. Due to my own positionality as a woman in midlife, and as an avid reader across the social sciences and humanities, I am fascinated by the diversity of narratives and how they illustrate the relationships between cultural geographies, narrativity, emotions and power (Sharp 2009). I am inspired by stories of Black midlife and menopause drawing on different forms of knowledge that fuse emotion, the character of age, mythology and new forms of resistance (cf Harding 1991). However, I begin with the popular narratives that call on the middle aged to adopt introspection or to fix themselves using neoliberal techniques.

Turning inwards and 'crisis'

Midlife as a stage of life has often been depicted as a time of reflection and introspection, and sometimes crisis. These are popular themes according to which characters in their middle years experience a period of dissatisfaction or restlessness, often leading to impulsive decisions or major life changes. One well-known example is found in James Hollis' (1993) *The Middle Passage* (and his other books), which explores the psychological aspects of midlife crisis. This book takes a typical Jungian psychology approach, delving into issues surrounding re-evaluation of priorities. To some extent, this approach views midlife – when ageing and mortality, career transitions and uncertainty come to the fore – as a time when people cannot or do not want to live with the cultural and social expectations they previously took for granted – or at least they did not reflect on themselves as being wrapped in social roles to the extent that their 'more authentic' selves were suffocating. The Jungian call for introspection is arguably one of the most widespread and popular motifs, and it was either directly (referring to books) or indirectly (referring to diluted ideas) referenced by my middle-class interlocutors over the years. What is geographically curious in these ways of narrating midlife is the contested idea of 'crisis' as directed inward instead of producing space outward, even potentially after the presumed 'inward work' has been carried out. In the meantime, Hollis insists that the Jungian concept of 'individuation' does not necessarily lead to self-centred, egoistic licking of wounds and regret of what has not been achieved outwardly; instead, Hollis sees individuation as a quest story for transformation (see Frank 1995) through the shedding of unsuited and unneeded social roles which have become obstacles to living a fuller life.

However, there are several problems with this type of crisis narrative. Very often, these musings ignore the fact that the majority of people in middle age are dealing with very practical uncertainties of life that are political, social and economic in origin. They are also sharply gendered and place-contingent. The very call for an internal shift grows from the internal agenda of 'the personal self-project', as Sheehy (1977; 1981) puts it. Yet, in crisis narratives, the tasks of generativity that other psychologists, such as Erikson (1980), call people to perform remain vague. Setiya (2010) sharply criticizes Sheehy's views and the success that writing about the midlife crisis brought in the 1980s. Setiya, drawing on large-scale surveys, dismisses this 'crisis' as almost non-existent, a buzzword without any basis, and yet he comes to contradict himself, at least to some extent. Although Setiya replaces the term 'crisis' with a more wordy description of some kind of privileged dissatisfaction, this turning point sees him arrive at largely the same conclusion as the Jungian, or crisis-oriented, genre of writing.

There are, nonetheless, several glimmers of hope in these introspective approaches. Drawing on the work of John Stuart Mill and on insights from Buddhism, Setiya (2010) states that in midlife, a more meaningful life can be found when a person turns their gaze to outward objects. This contributes to the shaping of some tools for generativity and space production, which are oriented towards others. Importantly, the discussion of crisis (climax as a dramatic change that bodies can experience), to some extent, reminds us that capitalist exploitative neuroses towards human bodies and social roles would always hit a wall, regardless of whether societies and businesses treat humans as objects that must or should avoid bodily ageing and social change (Jamieson 2022).

Argentinian psychoanalysts Montero, Ciancio de Montero and Singman de Vogelfanger (2019) do not dismiss the concept of crisis in midlife. Instead, they call for a serious consideration of the perception of time limitation and how people in midlife become conscious of the transience of life. Their introspective approach highlights the often-overlooked value of humanistic geographies – that is, our need to make sense of spaces, our space and time in the world and our spiritual needs in a material world (Stein and Niederland 1989). These authors also invite us to examine critically the mythologies that, for better or worse, have led some of the scientific approaches to midlife. One such example is found in Moore's (2022) historical analysis of the role of astrological climacteric years – with the seventh septenary (age 49) marking the female 'crisis' – in French male doctors' invention of the concept of menopause. Even better, these approaches should invite geographers and kindred spirit researchers to work with indigenous epistemologies that overthrow the ways midlife is generally talked about in Western imaginations (more on this at the end of the chapter).

Neoliberal anxieties and humour

Neoliberal male and female gazes on midlife – these do indeed tend to be gender binary – are pervasive in literature and popular science. Moreover, they tend to seep unreflectively into policy – be it work- or learning-related policies, policy ideas on successful ageing or public health policy – emphasizing that one is responsible for one's own success. Neoliberalism as a cultural idea revolves around individualism and the unsustainable and often a-spatial, a-temporal and a-historical imperative that says one must remain young to revive and reclaim self. As such, neoliberal anxieties justify Gullette's (2016) argument about youth-obsessed societies. Popular self-help books tend to blame the individual if they do not realize quickly enough that spells of disappointment and misery they experience are due to their own lack of self-sufficiency and stamina to transform these temporary thoughts. Here, ageing figures are caricatured as slipping into comfortable sneakers and a quiet life when they should be striving towards a new beginning. The suggestion is that after neoliberal work on self is done, a middle-aged person can become radiant, strong, powerful, like they were before but better. Books propose psychological reprogramming of the brain to tackle fear and insecurity, and there are step-by-step guides to turn dreams into reality, practical workbooks and action plans to navigate life after disorienting dips in midlife (Mathews 2016; Albertson 2021; Barton 2023).

One specific strand in these transformation stories (cf Frank 1995) tackles the sense of a turning point and decline in professional life, providing managerial advice on how to stay on top at work for the next two or more decades (Hulce 2020). There is no shortage of male self-help books either (Ochs 2015; Billings 2018; Scheinman 2022), encouraging deflated male power to do better, be stronger and take back power, as well as satirizing body anxieties, weight gain, the hair transplant industry and openness about suicidal ideation in midlife. These are progress and power stories from the male space in the world (cf Gullette 2016).

The youth-obsessed narrative leads us to the point of gendered humour, including some forms of nastiness. Many self-help books, films, podcasts and social media posts satirize the experiences and dilemmas faced by the middle-aged protagonist. The lens of physical signs – such as hot flashes, night sweats and emotional imbalance – is often employed. Some portrayals of midlife use humour to highlight the challenges and absurdities of how one should, or how one wants to, look, feel and perform when self-image and market pressures clash. However, while these portrayals can serve some purpose in illuminating free spirit and awareness of how the body and ageism work in society, as ageing and gerontology research has shown (cf Skinner et al 2015), we need to attend to the more oppressive forms that constrain agency and further stigmatize people. Moreover, unreflective satire and derogatory talk about bodies and middle-aged people's place in life are rather closer to studies which demonstrate how racism and ethnic othering work than they are to the self-liberating subversive laughter of elders.

I illustrate this using a comedy series, shown on Finnish national television on channel YLE, called *Hormonit!* (which translates as 'hormones') in 2023. This tells a fictional story in which the main protagonist is a gynaecologist. This character feels overwhelmed, tired and irritated and is caught snoring in the middle of the day by her young daughter. Following this, a sympathetic suggestion from a younger colleague leads her to contemplate on whether these could be menopausing signs. The protagonist then criticizes herself as 'old' and 'done', and tries to check her own 'egg reserve', a term doctors often use when referring to the functioning of ovaries (see Clancy 2022 for a critique of this practice and language towards people with ovaries).

The protagonist then takes leave to cope with 'burnout', a kind of code word in patriarchal environments, signifying that a person who is struggling at work cannot function efficiently and cheerfully enough to keep serving capitalist work schedules. She shouts at a man who tries to help and then shouts even more at a female receptionist at the gym ('the scales were wrong'), apparently to make the point that weight gain and irritability are common when menopausing. Life goes on with ups and downs, and she has hormone treatment, although, as realistically depicted, she finds it difficult to obtain one particular product in the place where she lives, and on top of that, she encounters a pharmacist who does not shy away from commenting on her prescription. The crudeness in the programme's depiction of biological aspects of menopausing seems to be intentional, and I was surprised at how uncritical the viewers' social media comments were – these were mainly women, and they tended to watch the series alone, though sometimes with their partners. However, there was no productive critique on how such a biopower caricature affects people and how it silences other ways of looking at midlife as an emancipatory project of solidarity and praxis to challenge and subvert patriarchal structures. Menopause jokes, of course, rely on ideas of male superiority and female exclusion, but there needs to be more conscious understanding of how women too participate in producing spaces of oppression through self-derogatory remarks, silences, coping alone and ultimately non-solidarity with so many others who need empowerment and social agency. Yet positive changes should be for the many, not just the privileged few.

Gullette (2016) explains that midlife novels have proliferated since the mid-1970s, with *progress* narratives dominating instead of the *decline* narratives that were common previously. This new vision, with its refocusing of midlife as a condition of possibility, was linked to demographic change, as it coincided with the period in the US and the UK the when the baby boomer generation transitioned into midlife. Neoliberal self-help books (similar to the TV series discussed earlier) continue this line, though their impact on progressiveness is arguable. They tend to treat midlife anxieties as diffused and unconnected with larger structures in society. Hence, the solutions they propose are individualized – for instance, psychologism, lifestyle change, supplements and medications. Rather than being progressive, these are narratives that expand the space of biopower, as Cranston (2017) argues based on her research on youth self-help books, where the focus is even more on physicality and rejection of ageing. Through Foucauldian neoliberal techniques, subjects are invited to work on their bodies and minds to fit into systems rather than changing them (Foucault 1991; Anderson 2011).

Oversharers, wise future elders and other space-makers

In contrast to the types of narrative discussed so far, there is a cluster of critical and emancipatory writing about midlife. Women have long been accused of being too open and emotional, and of having less rigour and cold objectivity than their male counterparts. Drawing on Zimmer and Hoffman (2011), Sykes (2017) makes a proposal that can help shed light on other ways of talking about midlife and the ways in which midlife narratives are dismissed. Her focus is on the accusation of oversharing. By analysing female writers and reviews of their work, she demonstrates how women have been labelled oversharers due to their autobiographical bodily, sexual and emotional insights. Numerous reviews and articles appearing after Chris Kraus' 1997 novel *I Love Dick* saw it as a feminist cringe comedy (Marso 2019), while others saw it as a private theory (Elkin 2015) or 'autotheory' (Farrant 2022). I read the Latvian translation of the novel, translated by the Latvian poet Agnese Krivade (Kraus 1997/2022). Sykes' (2017) point applies to this novel, as its reclamation of the female voice in order to share how and what the female writer desires is productive and emancipatory in breaking through the silences of midlife. It means writing 'herstory' as opposed to history (that is, 'his-story').

Krivade (2022), in her analysis of Kraus' (1997) book, refers to Eisler (1988), who contends that the rise of the patriarchy coincides with the production of written language. The feminist search for the self, hence, needs to be 'exhumated' from under the deep sediments of cultural space-making, which has created language and theories of exploitation, success and competition, burying respect for the body deep under its his-story (DeLyser and Shaw 2013: 505). Whether you hate or love the book and what Kraus did in using some real names, not to mention including her own real tears, frustrations and struggles, this novel is 'herstory', not oversharing. It shows, with explosive consequences, that women can write about how and what they want, in this case seen through the author's own unique midlife positioning. She took a real risk as a woman writing her story and 'talking back' to sexism and racism (hooks 1988). But of course the alternative of silence would lead nowhere anyway.

Another way of narrating midlife can be called 'becoming wise'. As an example, Blackie's (2022) *Hagitude* is not a counter-narrative to the rapidly expanding narratives of hormone treatment and medicalized menopause; rather, hers is a praxis of claiming life and home, of creating one's own space, mythology and habitats in midlife. Blackie's story portrays with burning emotional rage a beautiful reclaiming of living through her body. Hers is a story of claiming the value of becoming an elder in a society blinded by the illusion of youth, and of living through illness, as so many of us do, in an ableist world. This idea of becoming of elders provides a potent perspective (see also Loe 2011; Sandberg 2013) that still rarely surfaces among the hegemonic ideas of lifecourse theory and practice. Blackie's story makes peace with the classics most of us grew up with, such as de Beauvoir's (1949/2011) *The Second Sex*. Burning with rage can be a collective and transformative way to outgrow classic narratives which, while giving us a breakthrough to reference, failed to show that ways other than pathologizing female ageing are right in front of our eyes (or just next door; see Lulle 2018; Barry 2019; King et al 2019). While the archives of French male doctors were still comfortably dormant, not yet studied with a critical and skilful eye (Moore 2022), de Beauvoir's classic story remained limited. de Beauvoir's narrative was what Amini and McCormack (2019), drawing on their research in Iran, call the 'loss' narrative: with the chaos of their changing bodies, women operating in the constraining contexts of patriarchy and religion narrated their midlife as loss.

Blackie's (2022) narrativity is just one of many that exist apart from neoliberal capitalism's storyline of 'managing' midlife (see also Peterson and Kiesinger 2019, especially on transformative midlife narratives of illness). Blackie (2022) shows that rage can be a productive force. Scaffoldings of oppressive capitalism and patriarchy break loose in midlife and, unless we suppress anger at sociospatial and gendered orders, can give rise to emotional geographies (Davidson et al 2016; Pile 2010) anew. Pinkola Estés (1992), in *Women Who Run with the Wolves*, has already shed light on the centrality of the emotion of rage in space creation. Mythologies are space-time narratives that need to be uncovered for indigenous, racial and gender justice (Lawson 2011). When rage is lifted from individualized oppression to the potent collective action against patriarchal structures, it becomes a positive force for change. Anger can function as a 'wise teacher', driving change and providing strength to challenge orders that are otherwise taken for granted (Pinkola Estés 1992). The task is neither small nor easy in the current world, which continues to dictate women's places and perpetuates the decline in economic, racial and social justice. Women of colour and ethnicized women experience chronic illness, earlier mortality, persistent poverty and consistently lower wages; this is a situation that persists from the 1980s and 1990s, when classic midlife textbooks, such as Baruch and Brooks-Gunn (1984) and Lachman (2001), were published. Anger, in combination with autobiographical narrativity, made a difference on British television with the 2021 Channel 4 documentary *Davina McCall: Sex, Myths and the Menopause*. The documentary had a ripple effect that shattered the silencing consensus on how menopausing women are to be treated in the UK and beyond. As a result, visits to doctors soared and public media increasingly turned its attention to menopause issues.

In seeking other ways to narrate midlife, I drew strength from the multiplicity of standpoints that exist. I increasingly turn to Black feminist writing and critical pedagogies that support resistance against the grind of capitalist culture. One example of this resistance is the Rest and Resist movement coordinated by the Nap Ministry, which was founded by Tricia Hersey, a bishop, poet, narrator and inspiration to people to liberate themselves. As part of this movement, Black feminists organize collective rest sessions to reconnect with their ancestors and elders. They draw power from activists like Audre Lorde (1980; 1997) and others who nurture and share narratives of the written and spoken word, narratives of pain and joy, and praxis of overcoming oppression. Lorde championed what she called 'practiced intersectionality', because our skin, ethnicity, class, motherhood and sisterhood, sexuality, politics and living through illness all shape our spaces in the world.

Rest and reconnection across academic silos, rather than having to deal with yet another paper, conference or project, was what I was looking for to feel better in midlife. During the time when I could not write, inaction was necessary and productive, although in ways other than neoliberal academia expects our bodies to experience. I began to trust my body when it said that it needed space and time to rest. I was increasingly looking around for others who resist the grind, and I found the most inspirational and life-affirming standpoints among queer and crip studies. For instance, the Queermenopause Collective (nd) provides a path forward in ways that explore how networked, social agency can turn the tables on patriarchal oppression. I re-read the Boston Women's Health Collective's (2006) work on ethics of collective action to reclaim ourselves and our bodies. They nurtured what Appadurai refers to as social imagination 'as a collective practice and a capacity to aspire' (2013: 287). According to him, 'to aspire is a navigational capacity' (Appadurai 2013: 188), meaning it is differently distributed along lines of social difference, especially race, class and gender – and age. The Boston Collective came together in the 1970s after a health seminar proposing women had been systematically excluded, mistreated, underserved and, as the current hormone treatment activists across the UK–US axis repeatedly emphasize, gaslighted about their bodies and ageing. While many of the facts in the informative books by The Boston Collective have been updated or are now uncertain in relation to hormone treatment, the principles of their ethics are clear and enduring. These activist women educated millions of people across the US and beyond, not for profit but for the purpose of helping them navigate their lives and bodies better.

Conclusion

Women, and indeed all genders, should share the stories. Autobiographical bricolages are a powerful way of sharing, caring and space-making. We can learn from these stories to produce new sociospatial relationships with and around our bodies. Education about our bodies and about the practices we use to make time and space for our own and other people's bodies is an ongoing task that calls for dignity and realism in language and encourages informed action-taking, a non-exploitative midlife and graceful ageing. Hence, these groups advocate not leaning uncritically on ideas such as hormone replacement therapy, through which the medical industry attempts to medicalize bodies at the level of replacing something lost after menstruation has ended. The Boston Collective taught that there is no such thing as health insurance, because it is impossible to insure health. Though one can be medically uninsured or underinsured, and this difference exacerbates inequalities. I revised this text after re-reading their books and sage advice. They called for activism, political action and the politicization of menopause as the key way to tackle patriarchy, which seemed to be on the rise. Various activisms await further academic exploration (Boyer et al 2023).

THREE

Midlife Transitions: Body and Work

Introduction

In this chapter, I consider transitions in midlife. I show how midlife has been defined in research. I also provide insights from my research with middle-aged migrants in Latvia, the UK and Nordic countries, and non-migrants in Latvia, where most of my recent research has been conducted. I draw on the *Handbook of Midlife Development*, edited by Lachman (2001); in its tone-setting first chapter, Staudinger and Bluck (2001) muse on reasons for the relative paucity of theoretical research on midlife at the time. They came up with two main conclusions: it is not easy to define midlife through the notion of chronological age; and the margins around people's forties and fifties are very flexible, and people can have midlife lifestyles, economics and social outlooks in their thirties and well into their sixties.

Taking the first of Staudinger and Bluck's (2001) conclusions, it is clear that definition of midlife based on age is an oversimplification. And very similar discussions take place in research on youth and older age transitions. Chronological age and lifecourse transitions are relational. In the meantime, there has been a considerable shift in the definition of midlife in statistical practice, with the age range shifting so that the period starts and ends later, and, relatedly, shifts in academic discourses and everyday affairs. Thus the young are considered young for considerably longer – at least up to age 34 according to typical Eurostat (2020) datasets, or even up to 40 according to various policies. Then comes the middle, which leads to older age beginning somewhere close to people's sixties, although recently this too has been pushed into the seventies and eighties, clearly due to increasing longevity. The solution that Staudinger and Bluck (2001) propose is helpful: to look at midlife as two related and quite distinct phases, early midlife and late midlife. In chronological terms, this would be before and after one's fifties, because around the age of 50, for biological, social and economic reasons, people in typical Western lifecourses turn their focus to health maintenance and the potential onset of chronic conditions, since children are often (but not always) grown up, and older midlifers start seriously thinking about retirement plans and investments.

Staudinger and Bluck's (2001) second conclusion for the lack of theoretical research on midlife concerns the perception, by individuals and society, that the transitions within midlife are unproblematic. This perception is based on a comparison between youth, when people are trying to get into the job market and onto the housing ladder and establishing families, and older age, when retirement and health decline brings radical change. The authors did not propose a specific solution for this flawed idea of unproblematic lifecourses. This assumption, as I demonstrate, might be rather superficial, especially when it comes to people who are outside of the stereotypical image of midlife – that is, the relatively healthy and wealthy, sedentary middle class, who are doing well compared to others in midlife. Due to my keen interest in migrants and my research being carried out in not exactly traditional Western settings, I aim to illuminate blind spots when it comes to assumptions of unproblematic transitions.

In terms of work and home transitions, I look at the existing research from the viewpoint of the problematic ideal of a standard lifecourse in midlife. Standard lifecourse transitions are theoretically considered to take place in sequence, moving through education, learning job skills, embarking on a stable career, establishing a home and so on. Embarking on these transitions usually marks the beginning of adulthood (Arnett 2001). While this view originates from the relatively short period of the Fordist economy (Aboim and Vasconcelos 2020), it has such a profound influence on knowledge production that scientific language about standard lifecourse transitions remains hegemonic (Potter 2020). Further, the implied norms of a standard lifecourse in midlife – that it is the core of society, since youth is still 'becoming' (Worth 2009) while those in older age are ushered to the margins – remains poorly developed conceptually, and this obstructs ways in which significant changes in learning, career, relationships, migration, home life and more can be meaningfully embraced in midlife.

Empirical research on intergenerational social mobility shows that in Western societies, midlifers have achieved the peak of their careers and income levels (see, for example, the MIDUS study in the US context; see MIDUS nd). However, this work-life achievement can be destabilized through work role transitions (Mahler 2011), care responsibilities and crises, such as divorce or illness (Peterson and Kiesinger 2019). These experiences are sharply gendered, classed and racialized (Barrett 2005; Perrig-Chiello and Perren 2005) and contribute to precarity and poorer ageing (Grenier et al 2020). An assumption of stable working lives in midlife no longer holds strength, even in relatively sedentary contexts, and this assumption is even more disrupted in the case of geographical mobility. And yet, while lifecourses are de facto pluralizing, the pull to conform to an imagined standard is strong in planning, politics and the everyday imaginations and frustrations of 'normal' life. Hence, this chapter touches on, but goes beyond, now long-standing debates about non-standard lifecourse transitions versus standard transitions in midlife, seeking ways to recognize the constitutive mutuality of spatiality and temporality (Bailey 2009: 413; Worth and Hardill 2015).

Given all of this, there is no common and universally agreed definition of middle age. In often-used chronological terms, middle age roughly coincides with the period from one's mid-thirties up to older age, which keeps shifting in the globally ageing world. Thus, middle age follows the period of 'youth', conceptualized by current policies and research as somewhere up to the mid-thirties. But chronological age is a relational category – lifecourse is never based on age alone (Elder et al 2003; Hopkins and Pain 2007; Hörschelmann 2011). Lifecourse is generally considered 'an age-graded sequence of socially defined roles and events that are enacted over historical time and place' (Elder et al 2003: 15). In youth, transitions usually mark shifts from school to work, from odd jobs to a stable career, and to establishing one's 'home' (Arnett 2001). Midlife comes with intense work, care and relationships (Lachmann 2001), while older age is the post-work period. Critical themes in midlife are 'time orientation, the balance between work and relationships, and opportunities for growth and generativity' (Staudinger and Bluck 2001: 11). Further, some researchers divide adulthood into early, middle and advanced adulthood (for example, in psychology, Nemiroff and Colarusso 1990) or propose calling only the time before retirement a mid-course (for example, in sociological lifecourse studies, Moen 2003).

What I seek to illuminate further in the remainder of this chapter and in the next chapter is how life transitions play out sociospatially in midlife. I work through the themes of body and work time and spaces in this chapter, then examine home and relationships in the next chapter. However, prior to that, I want to specify how temporality, generational difference and agency play a role in individual and social agency and in the desire to live better.

The contingencies of midlife: temporality, generational difference and agency

As sketched out earlier, midlife as a chronological category is contingent, meaning that it shifts over time and across places.

For example, since the early 2000s, research and many national and European Union (EU)-level policies and statistics have shifted their definition of the end of youth from 25 to 29, 34 (Eurostat 2015; 2020) and even older. Similarly, the beginning of older age, which is often linked to retirement and average life expectancy, has shifted considerably from the age of 60 to the late sixties or even the mid-seventies (Ahmed and Hall 2016). Whatever remains in the shifting middle is regarded as (middle) adulthood. Current literatures on ageing lean towards including existing and limited midlife research (Moen 2003; Stockdale et al 2013; Ní Léime 2017; Lulle 2018; 2020; MacKenzie and Marks 2019; Turek and Henkens 2020; Wildman 2020).

A fundamental feature of middle age is that it is a 'sandwich generation', often with socially and culturally varied caring responsibilities towards both younger and older generations (Davis 1981). The lifecourse approach emphasizes work, care for others and relationships (Lachmann 2001). According to developmental psychology, critical themes in midlife are 'time orientation, the balance between work and relationships, and opportunities for growth and generativity' (Staudinger and Bluck 2001: 11). Along with these themes, I consider people's relationships and shifting chronological notions of midlife today.

Further, midlife, which is difficult to capture and so is flexibly defined in chronological terms, exhibits specific forms of human agency due to the focus on generativity – not just egoistically taking, but giving to enable better lives for others. Conventional ways of seeing human agency as an individual capacity (Gecas 2003) must be superseded. Agency in midlife and intergenerationally is better theorized as relational and interdependent (Durham 2008; Holloway et al 2019). It is through intra- and intergenerational interdependencies, contingent in time and space, and against the backdrop of structural barriers, that the balance between work and care can be pursued. In the scarce existing geographic theorization of agency in midlife, recent advances are to be found in studies of youth and family (Holloway et al 2019). These studies build on the pioneering feminist geographies of Katz (1993) and Massey (2005: 124), who strove to see agency as interconnections in space that form constellations of temporary coherences. Such coherences or synchronization (Bailey 2009) can be seen as meaning one's own free will to pursue goals in life are linked to, or cohered with, other people, in particular, children, partners and the older generation.

Midlife temporality and agency can also be expressed through the idea of diachronicity – that is, extending and weaving together experiences and aspirations past and future (Staudinger 1999). Temporal horizons therefore shift away from future-oriented youth (Lulle 2014a). Everything past, present and future comes together in the now. In the meantime, while imagining ageing futures has been difficult due to bias against older age (Jones 2011), I have found that future imagination is contingent geographically. Extending future horizons for one's life in older age means having some 'control over the next moment of time' (Morson 2010: 93). In my data, migrants and non-migrants, due to social security and cultural attitudes in the places where they lived (Latvia, Finland and the UK), had quite different orientations to future ageing (Lulle 2018; 2019). For example, while those in Latvia who had never migrated tended to avoid thinking about older age and retirement, UK-based Latvian migrants in their fifties were more positive about getting older and were preparing for retirement and actively imagining where and how they want to live when they retired. These comparisons were based on people with rather similar dispositions in terms of education and the work they do. They were not well off; those in Latvia tended to have an average income and those in the UK had rather small salaries in relative terms.

In addition, it is important to consider the idea of generativity versus stagnation in midlife – generativity offers a richer life and better understanding of self (Erikson 1980). Caring for others and giving are forms of relational agency, and Erikson maintains that living outwards – giving and generating value for other people, especially the younger generation – is the central task of midlife.

Body scale

We make sense of the world through our bodies. Body scale and materiality of body are fundamentally geographical in their ontology. We might ask: What is space and scale? What are relations (Ley 1977; Del Casino 2009)? By focusing on the body, we can advance knowledge on spaces, connections and temporalities (Schatzki and Natter 1996; Longhurst 2000; Rose 2007). I observed extensively in my recent research on midlife and ageing in Latvia how middle-aged people mundanely change their relationships with space.

An especially noticeable change was related to eyesight, with deterioration of near sight, or presbyopia, affecting ability to read, use digital devices and engage in close work. When I met people who I interviewed several years ago, some were now wearing glasses or would ask me to read a menu for them. As one of my interlocutors, Lienite, in her fifties, repeatedly said, she was at the age of 'long arms', meaning that without her glasses, she needed to read the menu at arms' length in order to make out the words. Not wearing one's glasses on social media was a ubiquitous way to order and control such midlife transitions privately and publicly. Inguna, in her early fifties, showed me not only how to take care not to have glasses visible somewhere at the edge of a photo but also how to take 360-degree pictures, because 'then people cannot zoom in on my face'.

These encounters with biological ageing and their sociospatial expressions are ubiquitous in midlife and relate to how people learn to adjust to their changing appearance and new sensory experiences. More seriously, encountering the first signs of ageing in one's own body may not only lead to health scares but also compound the difficulty of other common experiences in midlife, such as caring for ailing relatives, facing the death of loved ones and grieving. Health geographies in their current form – seeing life and health, and the practices people adopt to maintain health or deal with ill health, within the broad social environments where people live – are well-equipped to explain midlife transitions (Gesler and Kearns 2002). I begin here with insight, based on my research, on early midlife.

Generativity and embodied relations

Gunita and Aigars were both from Latvia; I interviewed and observed them in the UK over the course of a decade. When I first met them, they were both in their late thirties and divorced. They had established a family in the UK and were raising a child together. All three – parents and child – were healthy, and Gunita and Aigars wanted to provide the best environment they could for their child with the limited resources they had as educated migrants. They were climbing the income ladder somewhat more slowly than their British peers due to their lower starting point in typical migrant jobs – in their case, jobs in hospitality. Gunita and Aigars moved out of London, where raising a child was too expensive and buying their own property was not possible on their income. They settled in a town with a commute to London of around eighty minutes. The couple wanted to raise their child well, so they took out a mortgage to buy a house 'on the right side of the street', as Aigars put it. The house was considerably more expensive than their previous accommodation, which was nearby, but due to the allocation of school places based on postcode, the new location meant they were able to send their child to a better school.

Aside from this typical midlife consideration, the family's most common everyday quarrels were about food. Gunita was anxious about the way they ate, what they ate and what they taught their child about food. Generativity – giving to others – was clearly embodied and shaped by profoundly ubiquitous market pressures and discourses of good parenting and good nutrition for a healthy lifestyle. There were days when Gunita threw out most of the food in the cupboards and fridge, deeming it fast food, heavily processed and containing harmful preservatives. But after a couple of days, the cupboards would be full again, often with the same type of food. Every month or so, Aigars would take their child to McDonalds for fast food, and Gunita was very unhappy about this.

What this example illustrates is that body scale events are also relational and intergenerational. The body is a battlefield where marketing and other ideas clash (Simonsen 2000). Despite the stereotypical US middle-class conclusion about midlifers being in the 'prime of health and wealth' (cf MIDUS 2013), midlife households are strongly shaped by the broader neuroses and anxieties produced by markets, profit and lifestyle ideas, which sometimes emancipate people from guilt but often trap them so that they feel they are not doing enough to maintain their own health or that of their children.

Body changes

I propose that change in one's body is a key transition in midlife. Emotional factors, such as changes in body image, self-esteem and self-perception, can affect eating behaviours and contribute to weight gain during midlife, as multiple nutrition advice books and podcasts tell us. While these pressures, widespread in beauty magazines, were seldom a concern for the people I interviewed, they did surface occasionally. In one example, Ilze, a woman in Latvia who had never migrated, had been conscious of her body image all her life but in her forties, at around the time she encountered the first signs of ageing, she fell ill. Getting her health back was Ilze's priority, and for her this meant strenuous exercise and healthy eating, but she experienced difficulties getting back into work. 'Nobody wants to hire a fat person', she once told me. Body changes in midlife, which happen for various reasons, are relational as well as individual struggles. Ilze's changing body not only shattered her self-esteem but also affected her work chances and relationships. Ilze gathered as much information as she could, drawing on a combination of scientific sources and emancipatory writing on the subject of alternative medicine and lifestyles (cf Doel and Sergott 2003). Even so, her struggle was real, lonely and expensive, as many doctors dismissed her health concerns as simply resulting from being overweight. When she managed to reduce and stabilize her weight, Ilze said that her goal was to 'look good' for as long as she could. This is how the body as flesh becomes a contested social and political space (Schatzki and Natter 1996). Entwined with ageing bias is the dangerous neoliberal idea that our bodies are worthy only when they are slim, attractive and able. To counter this, we need to seek other ways of living, affirming life in the bodies we have. Hence, I argue that an emancipatory approach to the body in midlife should not stop at investigation of body image alone. People in midlife face real struggles and discrimination based on their bodies, when actually they contribute more to society through their combination of skills and considerable expertise (Infurna et al 2020).

Another example, from Norway, involves Ruta, a housewife who was married to a Norwegian man. When I interviewed her in her forties, she was happily busy with regular physical activity, but in the next interview, after her 50th birthday, she brought up the subject of weight gain. Ruta was furiously studying different schools of healthy eating and experimenting with the ideas she found. She insisted that buying and preparing balanced food for herself and her family was the biggest challenge in her life now. Despite the media discourses on female body beauty, Ruta was more concerned with her quality and ease of life. 'It is so much easier to live when you are lighter', Ruta said, looking back on the decade of her forties and musing on the emotional struggles that encounters with hormonal ageing bring for many women.

Body transitions and the process of ageing

For the women in my research, far more important than looks was a concern with maintaining health. This was evident when they spoke explicitly about menopause and when they talked more broadly about what they do to maintain their bodies. In the interviews I carried out before 2018, a few women mentioned menopause, but in more recent conversations, I noticed this subject was more normalized and the women talked about the compounding impacts of menopause on wellbeing. In an interview in Latvia in 2018, Anda, in her mid-fifties, brought up the topic of body changes herself when we spoke about ageing. She said:

> Of course, I feel it in my body. Hot flushes lasted for about five years. Sure, I did try to dress in layers, eat carefully not to trigger flashes, but anyway it was hard. For example, in the middle of a public talk, I got totally soaked and then shivered from chill.

She did not use hormone treatments, as her fear of what they could bring in terms of chronic illness and, potentially, early death was too high. Anda tried various herbal supplements, all in vain. Only after years of her body adjusting to the changing oestrogen level did she eventually experience relief. Anda's openness about her menopausing experience in 2010s Latvia should not be taken for granted, as this subject was rarely brought up by research participants. Silence on the issue was a social norm. Anda's experience can be counted as 'transitional': she recalled how her body changes started and how long it took to reach a kind of new 'normal', body-wise (cf Amini and McCormack 2019; see also Frank 1995).

Similarly, Skaidrite, a non-migrant who I interviewed in a small Latvian town in 2020, recalled how bodily experiences of menopausing changed her way of being in public spaces and how she learned new daily routines in order to live differently. Skaidrite told me that one of the most unpleasant experiences was when she went to a theatre in Riga and was drenched in sweat after experiencing hot flushes. She had no spare clothes with her to change into and she felt publicly embarrassed. This story can be linked to the long history of women's bodies in public places – bodies that are out of place according to the norms produced by male bodies (Longhurst 2001). However, she immediately turned the conversation to what she was able to do. She shared her self-knowledge and praxis: 'I paid attention to food and realized that spicy food, fried food, some soups, some drinks caused the hot flashes to be more severe. I learned to avoid these.'

I want to make an observation that complicates the idea of transition. Anda was older than me by 15 years or more. She shared experiences which may be ahead of me. This age difference – not enough to give the suggestion of a mother-daughter type of relationship – freed a space for us to talk and share insights in a woman-to-woman way. Skaidrite did not see her experience merely as a temporary transition; instead, she emphasized her new daily eating routines, which she maintained as a way of life and which also empowered her to make choices in life that made her feel better about her body (more in Chapter 5). Another research participant, Gaida, in her mid-fifties, did not mention menopause at all when I interviewed her in Riga in 2018. However, she emphasized that body care had become quite central in her life. She went to gym classes, changing routines and introducing more weights over time (see also Lulle 2018). Despite her dislike for weightlifting, Gaida said she had to do it for her bone health and to maintain muscle mass. These again were new routines which, even though Gaida disliked them, at least initially in her transition to body care, were seen as part of a new way of life and as part of the broader processes of change that midlife and ageing bring.

Taking action, but how?

In the previous examples, Gaida took action, as did Skaidrite. They changed their mundane routines. These changes, most often, were influenced by the widespread discourses of healthy living and techniques to maintain the body. Among the many products targeting people in middle age are so-called health supplements. The growth of complementary medicine further reveals how midlife is lived not only as an individual process with some indications of psychological transition, but also through consumerism.

I could not ignore the supplements market and the broader discourses on how people 'should' treat themselves to maintain health and wellbeing. In 2010, while gathering data for my doctoral work, I took a four-day road trip with a person who was shipping goods between Latvia and the Channel Island of Guernsey; among the packages being shipped were health supplements. The driver was somewhat wary of these: 'All those women's vitamins,' he said grudgingly, 'I told them [migrant women] that only unopened, sealed packages can be delivered.' I did not pay attention at the time to the expression 'those women's vitamins', so it escaped my notice whether or not these were hormone prescriptions (referred to by DeLyser and Shaw 2013: 505 as '"mother's little helper" pill'). However, I made a note in my field diary that there were energy supplements, such as ginseng. The women in my research took supplements like this in the hope of having more energy throughout the working day. Many purchased supplements from direct marketers. That industry often targets middle-aged people with no specific health concerns but a vague idea of wanting to do something to help their bodies.

Some of the men I interviewed were busy with vitamins and supplements too. Janis, who was 50 when I interviewed him in Guernsey more than a decade ago, told me firmly that he had decided to take his health into his own hands. He stopped drinking, looked after his diet and increased his physical activity, and more important for him, he also attached hope to purchases he made as the result of a massive direct marketing scheme. Janis showed me a large number of supplements he had bought, which were to be added to water to improve its structure and quality and thereby increase his calcium levels, eye health and more. Improving water quality was meaningful for him because he saw his consumption of the enhanced water as replacing harmful drinking (of alcohol) and he believed the water was an effective way for him to not only maintain health but also quickly purify his body. Latvian media have extensively investigated the businesses that provide such products and the extent of misleading claims about health benefits (cf Re:Baltica 2022).

This theme of hope in supplements played a large role in the life of another male interviewee who I spoke to in 2023 – Arvids, who was in his early sixties and working in the UK. Arvids left Latvia for the UK in his late forties and worked for a food packaging service. He initially worked erratic day and night shifts, but he learned that this was bad for his health and asked for night shifts only or day shifts only, so as not to mix up his diurnal rhythm. That fixed his tiredness, and he was healthy, aside from one recent episode when he felt chest pain and self-diagnosed a heart condition. While the experience was unpleasant, he did not feel scared or think he needed urgent care. 'So, I decided to walk on my own and admit myself to hospital', he said. After checks, he was indeed diagnosed with a coronary issue and given instructions to take pain killers, lower cholesterol and monitor his blood pressure. On reading the leaflets provided with the prescribed drugs, he realized that the drugs can have many negative side effects. At this point, he turned to supplements.

Promising literature is emerging on one the largest issues in migration and health – specifically why most immigrants arrive in excellent health but experience poorer health, compared to people born and living in the places where they move to, as they age; even second-generation immigrants are worse off (Rosenfeld 2004; Jang et al 2023; see also Torres and Hunter 2023 on mental health). Many factors are at play. Social determinants of health, including socioeconomic status, education, employment and access to healthcare services, can significantly affect the health of middle-aged migrants. In addition, mental health is a critical aspect of middle-aged migrant health and loneliness. However, what I have drawn attention to in this chapter is that the people I interviewed wanted to learn more about their health and wellbeing and to maintain it. The problem is that with the lack of easily accessible scientific knowledge, the market moves towards the highest profit, exploiting this generation. Arvids was initially sceptical when he first found information about very expensive Omega 3 oil products. He was highly educated and used to analysing information, but his own health problems, though not urgent, created a fertile space for his anxieties. He went back to the company advertising the products and started studying them more extensively. The intensity of our conversation changed considerably when he explained that he was overtaken by the details and promises of what these products could do. Arvids asked my age. When I replied, he assessed how long would it take for me to enter menopause. I saw this inter-gender openness between strangers as a result of the large shift in public discourse on menopause in the UK, which I had not previously observed, at least not as directly, in other European countries. The challenge, however, was that the openness of our conversation was a 'side effect' of the use of middle-aged bodies for marketing purposes. The products he was interested in were very expensive. In sum, he was caught between anxieties about ageing and his wish to maintain his health, highlighting the point I made in Chapter 2 about neoliberal anxieties. Global-scale market producers profit from the anxieties that manifest in middle-aged bodies. Yet, the space which could promote a culture of productive, evidence-based knowledge, not driven by profit, still remains rather small, as middle-aged people are omitted from socially oriented theoretical and empirical interest.

Work: spaces and temporalities

Work transitions are not new in midlife theories. However, I seek to uncover how these transitions feel for people today and how they make sense of them. Extant midlife research is generally situated within the conversations on ageing, with the focus either on work in the distinct period before retirement (for example, see MacKenzie and Marks 2019 on professional reorientation; see also Moen 2003) or as a critique of ageist exclusion in the labour market (Turek and Henkens 2020). According to widespread general assumptions, (sedentary) people are often seen to have peaked in their careers and income levels in middle age. This is evident in, for instance, the MIDUS data in the US context, which covers the period from 1995 to 2013 (see MIDUS nd). However, the world's population has changed since this research; in many Western countries, people in middle age will soon be the largest cohort. Migrants, at the time when they make a move to a new country, are usually younger, on average, than the population that already exists in their new country, but they inevitably transition to middle age. Overall, the size of the middle-aged generation will rise rapidly and significantly due to unprecedented population ageing in the 21st century (Vollset et al 2020).

Most of my Latvian research participants were young when political change began in the crumbling Soviet Union. Titma (2004) and colleagues have researched cohorts born in the Soviet Union in the 1960s. In their Path of the Generation since 1982 project, they a used longitudinal approach with several waves of data collection and analysis. This captured how respondents rebuilt their lives during the transitional post-socialism period. The key finding from this study relates to place and the political and economic systems. Titma (2004) claims that more people in the Baltic states than other post-Soviet states took advantage of the market system in their youth. This research, however, does not provide more nuanced insights into diversity and unequal opportunities on social and spatial scales. In my research, I have found that in the post-Soviet context of Latvia, work in midlife provides a curious case, with more diversity than classic lifecourse theories predict. At the same time, my insights into the lives of people in and from Latvia also link to postcolonial contexts, where migration is an aspiration. Further, in more sedentary contexts, which provide the un-challenged norm for most quantitative studies of midlife and work (such as the MIDUS study; see MIDUS nd), migration adds nuance to why and how people want to change jobs or get stuck in jobs due to being in midlife. Hence, migrant employment is a useful lens to challenge standard lifecourse transitions using destandardization in lifecourse theories. Standard lifecourse transitions, albeit clearly criticized in more recent quantitative studies (Aboim and Vasconcelos 2020), have profound influence on knowledge production in geographies of midlife and remain hegemonic in the study of significant career changes in midlife (Potter 2020).

In Latvia, as in many other post-socialist countries, fundamental geopolitical changes have occurred that have necessitated non-standard lifecourse transitions, resulting in a greater diversity across lifecourses (Mayer 2004; 2009). But even in Western contexts, the destandardization hypothesis has reached saturation. It is this 'paradox of coherence' in social structures and policies that makes up the macro context for tensions in the lives of the middle aged. The overwhelming majority of migrants who hit the road in midlife are moving to catch up with the structural standards of an imagined 'normal life'. The measure of their achievement is almost always a comparison to back home – that is, having a better, more stable life than they would have had if they never moved (Lulle 2023). They key domains around this tension are work and home. In the remainder of this section, I analyse the typical ways in which work spaces and temporalities unfold, drawing on the lives of the migrants I interviewed, but also using sedentary lives to produce context.

Power and growth

Next, I provide three examples of how the middle-aged take power and experience professional growth. Each relates to geographic mobility.

For women, intergenerational timing, meaning, the age of children and care duties towards them, is crucial. Agate, a Latvian woman, in her early sixties when I interviewed her in 2023, had been a highly accomplished international worker and had retired early. She could do so thanks to the international organization she worked for: not only did it provide a good salary and saving opportunities, but it had a pension scheme that was much more beneficial than typical private sector or government jobs. In addition, she was almost fully medically insured for the rest of her life – another important benefit of her retirement package, which she took advantage of for wellbeing and health maintenance.

Agate had worked hard all her life. She was a high achiever in a government career during the Soviet period. After the collapse of the Soviet Union, when Latvia regained independence, she retrained and constantly updated her professional and soft skills (including language proficiency). She worked internationally for several organizations and also raised children. At the age of 50, took an opportunity to work abroad in a job that was a great career leap, but very demanding as it required a high level of personal and professional learning. She recalled that the timing was perfect. She was no longer needed for hands-on care of her children, who were already out of the house. In terms of her relationship with her partner, both were already used to living separately for long periods. She worked on three continents, calling this period her highest achievement by far. The job gave her a platform to become a senior professional internationally and use capabilities she had had all along but could not fully realize when her children still needed a considerable amount of care and stability in one country (see also Gecas 2003 on self-agency in midlife).

Similar to Agate, Zaiga, another Latvian woman, was around 50 when she got a major appointment as an international consultant. Again, the timing was just right because her children were finishing secondary school and preparing to leave for university life abroad. Her husband did not object, and the company covered an agreed number of journeys so that the couple could meet from time to time. However, in Zaiga's case, the job did not work out so well. Her children went through rough times, she experienced ill health, which led to difficult moments, and she did not have meaningful relationships with her superiors due to the highly competitive work environment (cf Knoll and Schwarzer 2002). She returned to Latvia, and one of her children, now adult, moved into her household as she needed familial support due to illness in their family and also because she wanted to see her parents more often (see Davis 1981 on the 'sandwich generation' and Holloway et al 2019 on relational agency).

The third example relates to Imants, in his fifties when I interviewed him in 2023. He was a Latvian working in a Nordic country on large-scale infrastructure projects. Imants had a technical education, obtained during the Soviet period, although in Latvia he had worked as a baker. Yo-yoing between jobs in unrelated professions was not unusual in the turbulent post-Soviet period. The bakery where he worked was close to his country home, and he also took care of the agricultural household. Then he got a job in Norway, and by the time we met he had been travelling back and forth for 18 years, with the trips booked and paid for by his employer. He usually spent up to three months in Latvia and three months abroad. During this time, a second child was born in his family in Latvia, as his wife continued with an administrative job. Imants' wife liked her job, but it did not pay well ('it is her hobby',

Imants said). As well as working, she took care of the house and children. Imants, in the meantime, experienced significant growth in terms of his career and salary. He learned to work with new technologies and took on responsibilities for large infrastructures. Most of his colleagues were from the Baltic states or other former Soviet republics, also middle-aged and educated during the Soviet period. He was thinking of retiring early. 'I have enough money for all our needs', he said, echoing what Moen (2003) calls 'mid-course', the time before retirement. Imants did not mean full and formal retirement, but rather working less intensely than he had been in the past two decades. Job opportunities were never far away for him. He was skilled and licenced to work with large infrastructure and to drive special equipment, so he was also in demand during his rest time in Latvia. I have come across this confidence to 'retire' from intense work in midlife in only a few other cases over my years working with Latvian migrants. One case was a highly skilled woman in early midlife, who was married to an Englishman, also highly skilled; both left their jobs to travel around the world for a year. Similarly, another woman, this time in late midlife, who was working in simple retail jobs in Guernsey, went on a nine-month trip with her newly retired British partner. They did not worry about having to find jobs when they returned home. They rented out their houses while they were travelling so that they would have extra income.

In the cases of Agate, Zaiga and Imants, the support and systems provided by the organizations they worked for was key to their professional growth. Such systems enable workers to put into practice the perceived ideal of a linear – upward – career path (cf Potter 2020; see also Titma 2004). However, although these systems are crucial in several ways that are specific to midlife, being within such systems does not always lead to success, as personal factors, like illness and relationships with superiors, can get in the way. However, in the three examples discussed, growth was both outwards (geographically) and upwards (socially). Aside from having good organizational support (for example, to help build savings and retirement funds), Agate, Zaiga and Imants had job security within their organizations (this suggests a privileged case of global social protection; see Levitt et al 2015).

For those who want to go travelling, having savings and property means that this lifestyle, widely depicted as adventurous, is possible. However, this is still rare among middle-aged Latvians living in the UK. Another important factor in people deciding to leave work to travel is having confidence that their skills and the relevant labour market will be strong on their return from travelling. Power and growth in midlife, in sum, are related to subjective sense of freedom to do what one desires and also to relative or emerging upward social class position.

Laying low

'Laying low' in relation to work time and spaces during midlife – that is, doing just what is required in the job and waiting for retirement – was far more common than the cases described earlier. Many of the middle-aged people I interviewed, especially women, at some point in their more mature midlife, realized that they would have liked to have had more responsibility at work and more knowledge and access to resources in order to climb the career ladder; however, few had been able to do this. When I spoke to Agate (one of the cases introduced earlier), she reflected on an acquaintance who was also highly skilled and accomplished when they worked together in government jobs in Latvia. She said that her former colleague, in her late fifties, has been laying low, but new reforms came into effect in the organization where she worked and her ideas and work were overturned by a new generation of civil servants. Agate did not pity her, but rationally concluded that the culture of growth in the international organization she worked for was in stark contrast to the structure for experienced professionals working in Latvian government jobs.

Laying low, indeed, was by far the most typical tactic I encountered in my research over the years. It was particularly pronounced in public sector jobs in the sedentary context. The narrowness of Fordist-type specialization also prevented people from deliberately changing professions in midlife (Aboim and Vasconcelos 2020). Even if people wanted to change jobs, the felt that they did not have the skills or flexibility to do something different. This hesitation demonstrates the hegemony of ideas about linear lifecourse transitions and how they affect people's decisions in midlife (Potter 2020). For example, when I interviewed Raita in 2018, she was working in polygraphy. Although she wanted to change profession, she was hesitant to do so because she worked in the same field all her life and she thought she did not have the skills to make a radical move. However, her job situation changed after a couple of years, as she was laid off. This external driver acted as catalyst for Raita, prompting her to take a different type of job. This can be interpreted as a move that goes against the hegemony of narratives that radical change in midlife work is too risky. Raita spent her last years prior to taking her pension developing skills in the non-government social sector. In 2023 she combined her pension income with volunteering and was content with the path she had taken, even though she had previously been hesitant to do so.

Being stuck in one place – a geographic location or a workplace – was also the most typical way that migrants experienced work in midlife (see also Lulle 2018). When Latvia joined the EU, many people embarked on transnational migration, travelling back and forth between Latvia and the countries where they worked. For those in midlife, working stints abroad were often motivated by the wish to earn money for some specific target, mainly to improve living conditions back in Latvia. The key motivator was to be able to invest in a property (more in the next subsection). However, the money people could earn in one or two years abroad was usually much less than they imagined. The economy was booming in Latvia in the mid 2000s, but inflation soared and there was a major financial crisis during 2008–2011. People's dreams became more expensive to realize, as with the passage of time, more work was needed to maintain properties. It was not enough just to change windows in a flat or replace the roof of a house – yet more money was needed for other renovations, or more savings had to be used up to rent an apartment while the work was going on, or the children needed support, and so the expenses piled up. The main reason why people ended up being 'stuck' abroad was the realization that retirement income is vital for secure ageing in Latvia (Lulle 2018). The current institutionalization of old age pensions significantly immobilizes people. For instance, migrants working in the UK often need to work for at least ten years there to qualify for a limited state pension (Official Statistics Portal (Latvia) 2023), though in comparison to the Latvian context, where the average state pension was €450 per month in 2023, the UK state pension may appear rather decent. To give some context, prices for daily expenses, such as food, can be even higher in Latvia and the UK. Furthermore, most of medical expenses for older people are covered by the NHS in the UK, which is not the case in Latvia.

Laying low, in sum, is the manifestation of the power of place and the institutionalization of lifecourses, which on the one hand provide stability but on the other create considerable barriers to change in one's working life in midlife. Importantly, stability is created for the benefit of organizations and employers, whereas for employees, stagnation is often the result.

Deliberate change

Some do change their working lives around the age of 50, deliberately and radically. While work-life changes in early or early midlife are well documented, studies usually focus on incompatibility of work and care schedules or reinventing work trajectories in a new place (see, for example, Haasler and Hokema 2022 in the context of working mothers in Germany and Schroot 2022 on migrant women). Next, I provide an example, drawing on the experience of Uldis, of deliberate change in midlife. The change described applies in two contexts – when Uldis was living in Latvia and when he migrated. I have known Uldis for more than a decade, having followed his lifecourse during his emigration to the UK, the Netherlands and Iceland. When I interviewed him in 2023, he was in his early sixties. Uldis had a higher education qualification in natural sciences, and he worked in Latvia in a related profession until the Soviet Union collapsed; then, he changed jobs to become a journalist. He left that job when he was 50. In Uldis' words, 'it was too stressful. I could not cope with the stress and the stream of events. I somehow felt that it was the right time for me to leave. No regrets.'

The background to the ease with which he left his job is important. He had recently inherited a house, he had modest savings, enough for a few months, giving him peace of mind that he could manage for a time. But, most importantly, he felt that he wanted to, and could, change the rhythm of his work. There were plenty of job offers for seasonal work in the UK or the Netherlands, where he could earn more and where he would have a radically different working life – that is, working with the body instead of with intellectual stress. This was not an uncommon observation throughout my years of research with Latvian migrants. Middle-aged women, in particular, stated that they could not cope with rigid schedules or that they needed to free their minds. They would often opt for a physical job abroad (Lulle 2014). After short stints in packing and agriculture jobs abroad, Uldis recovered his life-long passion: preparing food. He gained a vocational qualification for adults and became a baker. After working briefly in his new profession, he went abroad and worked as a chef until he qualified for a pension abroad. Not only was he happier in his new job, but he also learned new ways of living, gained exposure to different cultures and was able to finish a major renovation on his large house. Uldis did not see his professional change as deskilling in midlife (see also Moroşanu et al 2021 on medium-level education jobs and satisfaction among younger migrants). On the contrary, he saw his multi-profession lifecourse journey as a 'blessing'.

Opting for flexible schedules and finding work that builds on hobbies provided job satisfaction for both those who were sedentary in midlife and those who had migrated. Picking up skills in carpentry, tailoring, cooking, hairdressing or massage was common among the people I observed. There were two main reasons why these work choices provided satisfaction. First, people wanted to have their own work schedules: even if the need for flexible work was not dictated by duties of care, enacting agency over one's work schedule in midlife was perceived as important. Second, developing a hobby as a side job helped people cope with stagnation in their main job, in which people often needed to stay to qualify for pensions in the near future. This stability allowed people to learn new things through hobby-motivated creativity that was part of their daily routine, rather than as tasks imposed by an employer (Stenning et al 2021).

Two examples illustrate the point. Anita, in her late fifties, was working in various semi-skilled jobs in a small town. She had never migrated and never had enough savings to change her work radically. In early midlife, she had significant care duties for two children and a chronically ill husband. Only after her husband died was Anita able to create more space and time in her life to do what gave her joy, which represents one of the 'markers' of midlife (Brooks-Gunn and Kirsh 1984). Still working in a low-paid municipal job, she started to charge for her hobby, cake baking. Initially this was only for friends, but soon the word spread about how good her cakes were and her clientele increased. This pleasurable work boosted her self-confidence. She learned to drive in her early fifties, and her horizons expanded rapidly. Hence, doing a job one likes, even if it cannot provide a living and still requires one to keep an existing job, can become a viable tactic to live a more outward and satisfying life in midlife in the geographic context of a small town with limited opportunities for growth. Anita's was not a 'yo-yo' transition (Du Bois-Reymond and López Blasco 2003); rather, she created an expansive work life while simultaneously following the path of more routine work in her existing job.

A second example is found in the experience of Renate, who I have known for more than a decade. She was in her mid-fifties when I interviewed in in 2023. She had been a housewife in Latvia when her children were small. However, she had always been eager to learn something new: first she learned to buy and sell stocks on the stock market. The income she received was small, as she did not invest much, but the satisfaction of working alongside being a housewife was her main driver. Then her husband left her rather suddenly in her early midlife. She went to work in Ireland and the UK, and mainly did jobs to earn money so that she could provide education for her children and buy a flat in Latvia so she would have minimum life security in the form of a place to live. After an unsuccessful return to Latvia, working in a low-paid shop job that was neither stimulating nor rewarding, she opted for a live-in care job in the UK, which allowed her to move back and forth between countries. After feeling stuck and lacking perspective in Latvia, she was far more hopeful and satisfied with these new arrangements. The main thing that she emphasized in our conversations was her ability to choose when she would go to the UK (as she had agency over work schedules) and when she could take a longer time to rest in Latvia. Decades ago, Lopata and Barnewolt (1984) stated that life satisfaction is different for those who have stable jobs and those who are in flux in midlife. Renate's case opposes these findings. Unlike the stereotyped views of care jobs as menial and hard, Renate saw the job as a basis for personal growth, which had not been available to her before. She learned intensely and regularly how to care for the elderly in the intimate environment of home spaces, and she had considerable time for herself, which she spent on what could be called 'life-wide learning', doing new courses through micro learning platforms, not for money but to enrich herself. Formenti and West (2018) call this a rich and creative composition of learning through the lifecourse, where life experience is valued and enriches professional learning.

Conclusion

This chapter dealt with literatures on bodies and work midlife. This time in life has been perceived as rather unproblematic as it does not involve the dramatic life transitions faced in youth – such as leaving education, establishing a career and making a home – or the transition in older age from work to retirement. However, literatures on midlife do describe some transitions, which are usually related to crises in relationships, work or health (Peterson and Kiesinger 2019). The problem is that the plurality of midlife and its lifecourses gets overlooked in such approaches. Furthermore, most of the theoretical approaches consider midlife as a sedentary time by default. I have analysed transitions from two innovative angles. I use data gathered through my work with migrants and those who have not migrated but experienced significant geopolitical changes where they lived. I approached transitions in midlife through the body scale – which so far has also been rather neglected in lifecourse approaches – and through workspaces. Division of midlife into two rather distinct periods of life – early and mature midlife – is useful here, as this helps illustrate both bodily and work transitions and flexible boundaries of midlife (Baruch and Brooks-Gunn 1984; Staudinger and Bluck 2001; Hawkins and Haapio-Kirk 2023).

I argued that the body scale, in particular gendered embodiment, is a valid justification for midlife transitions. The distinction between early and mature midlife matters here. For example, in early midlife, care is often more oriented towards children's bodies. In later midlife, many care for ailing parents while their own bodies require extra attention too. I demonstrated how widespread ideas of what is good for the body, especially what we eat to build and maintain good health, intertwines with the midlife task of generativity. In other words, parents want to care for and enable good life habits in their children, and they want to be healthy and strong themselves in order to deal with the work and care tasks that midlife entails. Insights into how everyday life unfolds through the focus of body and generativity (not only our own bodies but those we care about) provide fascinating home, food and intergenerational geographies that need to be embraced and analysed.

Gendered ageing, and especially encounters with signs of menopausing, are relevant transitions. Hence, geographic interest in temporality and body has much to offer midlife studies. Yet, these are not only transitions but also larger processes that are social, cultural, economic and even political. There is a lack of both knowledge and public fora where body changes in midlife are discussed using evidence from research and where subjectivities are taken seriously. Such knowledge and engagement could influence the ways people live and how they use their spaces and time. I also drew attention to how widely market-driven businesses affect the lives and actions of middle-aged people, illustrating this point with insights into the level of trust placed on health and food supplements. Feminist economic approaches could be applied to supply and demand for supplement industries in relation to the middle-aged body. This could take research further and reveal how bodies, markets and desires shape the way we live in midlife.

In terms of work, the term 'transition' is not usually the most appropriate to describe the changes people go through in midlife (Lanchman 2001). There are transitions when change is deliberate (cf Gecas 2003), for instance, with the person making a conscious decision that the work they are undertaking is not a good fit for their current lifecourse. There are transitions to a different work and place through migration, and people transition to other jobs due to precarity or layoffs. However, a better overarching approach, potentially, is to view work in midlife as a process that reveals an array of interconnected scales: from body needs and desires to local and national economies and transnational networks for work. Again, due to flaws in the existing theory that sees midlife as an unproblematic period of life in terms of care and work, place-making and time use experiences need to be explored further. I invite such research, and I have provided insights into how people desire job changes, how they accomplish this and why many 'lay low' despite unsatisfactory jobs. The processual, rather than transitional, approach is also applied in the next chapter, where I focus on the domains of home and relationships.

FOUR

Midlife Transitions: Home and Relationships

Introduction

In this chapter, I analyse two key processes that unfold in midlife and are specifically shaped by midlife, namely processes related to home and relationships. Key literatures emphasize the latter but not the former. Due to my engagement with migrants in my research, the relevance of home is immediately obvious. This was one of the central processes, if not the key process, in the lives of most of the research participants.

Since Latvians who are currently middle aged have experienced dramatic changes in the economy and property regimes, the broader structural factors related to the historical period they have lived through are highly relevant to understanding their individual experiences of home. During the Soviet period – that is, from 1945 until 1991 – private property was restricted: few people owned houses and even those who did needed to privatize and re-register their properties after the Soviet Union collapsed. Denationalization and privatization shaped home ownership and changed lives in what we could see as class processes, following Western theories (Lulle 2023). Denationalization means that previous owners or their ancestors could reclaim real estate and land owned before the Second World War and the Soviet occupation. This process led to significant changes in living conditions for most people: owners gained important capital, even if the houses they got back were dilapidated and required significant renovation. Others became tenants and were subject to radical change in rental prices, which meant that many could not afford rents or that they had to leave denationalized properties. Privatization certificates were issued, based on how long people had worked under Soviet rule and on their age (that is, certificates were lifecourse related). All participants in my research on midlife were children or teenagers when these processes took place. Hence, their positioning in terms of property ownership or rental was shaped by these political and economic changes along with, for some, opportunities to inherit a house or a flat in midlife. Therefore, not only work but also, crucially, home ownership arrangements contributed towards security or precarity for this generation (Grenier et al 2020). For many of them, achieving the theoretical transition of youth by establishing their own home (cf Arnett 2001) actually happened in midlife and was a long process shaped by the historical context and individual lifecourse factors. Mass emigration or deliberate engagement in transnational migration were also deeply shaped by the desire to earn and purchase a flat or a house, as I describe elsewhere (Lulle 2018; 2023).

In terms of people's relationships, it is important to consider multidirectional processes, not only – as the early literature claims (Lanchmann 2001) – transitions, such as divorce, conflict and other unsettling events I want to demonstrate how care and relationships are contingent on – in other words, shaped by – time and space. Relationships are also networked (Ryan 2011) across the transnational space, and lives are linked (Findlay et al 2015) at various scales and temporalities. This means that people are connected to each other across their lifecourse. In midlife, earlier connections and closeness to parents can be reinforced, and places such as home, workplace and localities where people live can be reordered due to the links that people have with each other. Home, as I show next, is central to relationships in midlife.

Home

Home is missing in extant midlife theories. There are just few references in the literature, and these warn about the detrimental effects of home insecurity in midlife (for example, Robinson and Moen 2000; Bhat et al 2022). Home is fundamental to changes in family structure, space requirements, proximity to schools (especially in early midlife), amenities, mortgage possibilities, taxation and housing affordability (cf Baxter and Brickell 2014; Blunt 2005; Blunt and Varley 2004; Blunt and Dowling 2006; Soaita and Searle 2016). Home ownership in late midlife can intertwine with retirement planning during midlife. However, the culture of retirement planning (or not planning) is relevant too. I propose that home and lifecourse come together on a temporal horizon where people assess and make decisions according to institutionalized lifecourse ideas of what people in different life stages do and how they live, related to their ability to navigate jobs, care and income (Amrith 2022). These considerations revolve not only around jobs but, crucially, home too. In this chapter, I provide relevant insights from over a decade of research with people in middle age. I begin with the example of a couple in early midlife who built a house for the family, followed by the case of a woman, also in early midlife, who sought a move from the country to the city. Then I describe some experiences related to home in late midlife.

Young midlife: house ownership

Inese and Davids are both in their early forties. I have known the couple for more than a decade; my visit to their home in Latvia is a nice reunion for the three of us. The couple has two teenage children, who live almost independently on the second floor. Both Inese and Davids have lived and worked in Scandinavian countries, where the children were born. Inese takes the lead in telling the story of how they built a house for the family. 'Ever since I experienced living in a Scandinavian type of house, I wanted [to have one] for us', she told me. The couple owned a three-room flat in a block house, built during the Soviet period in Riga. But living with two children in a post-Soviet-type flat after their experiences in Scandinavia made them feel as though they had not fully transitioned from youth to adulthood. The couple wanted to have the best of the lifestyle and home experience they had in Scandinavia, as they felt that the Nordic approach was the 'good life'. The development task of generativity (Erikson 1980) shaped their actions towards home building – they wanted to achieve this so that their children would have the best experience possible in Latvia, incorporating the cultural and material expressions they enjoyed in Scandinavia. Hence, I argue, geographical attention to lifecourses is vital, because these unfold in specific places and involve materiality and ideas that are woven together through personal experiences or dominant discourses in society on what a good home is, implying middle-class home (Lulle 2023).

The couple crafted a plan. They moved out of their post-Soviet-type flat and rented it out to generate extra income so that they could purchase a plot of land for the house. Capitalizing on the notion of 'young family' – a trope widely used in social solidarity movements and policies, even if sometimes only as lip service – they moved in with an aunt; her flat had just two rooms, but she had a 'warm heart' and was willing to help the family. As Inese recalled, 'For about two years, all four of us lived together in one walk-through room. I remember that time as mainly being in bed, working on the computer, blogging about how we were planning our house. Everything revolved around the bed.' They persevered, mobilizing support from their parents and even neighbours in the form of interest-free loans and childcare. The final step was to sell their flat to reach the amount they needed for the house. Although the real estate market was passive at the time, Inese, with her skills in presenting the flat's interior as a clean and minimalistic Nordic-style space, got a client from a Nordic country who wanted to purchase the flat for her child, who had just begun studies in Riga. Inspired by the Nordic look of the flat, the client paid a price well above market average.

As soon as Inese and Davids were in their new house, which they decorated in the Nordic style they liked, including planting a Swedish cherry tree by the terrace, they both set out to improve their careers. Davids became an entrepreneur, while Inese started working for an international company; they each almost tripled their previous income. Both of these middle-class high achievers strongly linked the change in their lives to the way they felt and the lifestyle they had in their new house.

A few years after moving into their new home, Inese's sister bought a house nearby. Davids' parents had retired and were still living in a block house not far away, illustrating spatiality and geographical proximity of linked lives (cf Findlay et al 2015). They were getting weaker, had plenty of free time in retirement, and Davids wanted to have them closer by. They purchased a plot of land near their own home and built a summer house for Davids' parents. Later on, Inese's grandmother, who lived in a remote part of the countryside, started experiencing intermittent health issues, but travelling more than 150 kilometres to see her was difficult for Inese, given her other commitments (cf Baldassar and Merla 2014; see also Stockdale et al 2013). Emboldened by her capacity to build a home and bring together a network of significant people (her sister and Davids' parents), Inese sold her grandmother's house and bought another house for her, much closer to the family. In sum, this case illustrates an ideal type that characterizes desires and ideation in Latvian society of how a 'successful' midlife should look. This is also an example of how people learn neoliberal capitalism and lean on moral responsibilities (cf Smith 1994) of relatives and acquaintances instead of on the state.

A gendered move to the city

In this section, I argue that mid-lifecourse is not only about relationships with other people – family in particular (see

Stockdale et al 2013) – shaped by historical time and timing in individual lifecourses, but also shaped by agency (Elder 1994). I want to describe an experience during midlife that was motivated by self-actualization.

Ingrida moved from Latvia to Finland in her late twenties after meeting her future partner via an international dating app. Her previous higher education in Latvia was of little use in the Finnish labour market, so she raised two children and embarked on a new professional degree in Finland. The family lived for about a decade and a half in the countryside. Ingrida's husband climbed the career ladder, commuting to work in the city while she took care of the country house and their children and had a paid job in a small town too. It was when she was in her early forties that their two children, born a year apart, started showing talents that could be further developed in a city school.

When speaking about this, Ingrida initially organized her narrative around the needs of her children – specifically, she relied on the dutiful and celebrated task of midlife, caring for and developing others. However, she later revealed how draining and isolating life in a remote place had been for her. The house belonged to her partner's family, and it held meaning for him. Ingrida's extended family was in Latvia, and the house did not have the same significance for her; rather, it was a source of constant work and care. More so, although fully integrated into Finnish society, along the formal lines of language, family and work, when she reached her forties, she felt a shift as she became drawn towards the broader community of her ethnicity and the events and routines people shared, which in Finland was accessible only in the capital city.

She expressed the wish to move, but her partner was initially against it; he told Ingrida that she might not be able to find a job and was worried about how they would pay the rent on a city flat. Gendered spatiality becomes visible here: Ingrida's quiet life in the countryside created a comfortable scenario for her partner, who could enjoy work in the city and frequent work-related travel as well as a well-kept country house. But

Ingrida was ready for the move, with or without her partner. This gave her the emancipatory agency that is characteristic to midlife ideation but hard to achieve in existing gender and family relations. She employed what Amini (2023) calls 'tactics' of feminist action (see also de Certeau 1984). In Western contexts, agency is understood as free will and the capability to enact one's own will, and with this in mind Ingrida was drawing on social agency (Holloway et al 2019) and timing in her linked lives with the children (cf Elder 1993; 1994; Findlay et al 2015). When the children were at the age when they could change to a school that could support their talents, Ingrida announced to her partner that now was the time for the whole family to make a move.

While classic theories of midlife (cf Lanchman 2001) emphasize ruptures as turning points in relationships, I want us to consider how much more complex mid-lifecourses are and how not only linkages, places of living and historical period shape them, but also how people enact their agency to move to a different place. We have a good reason to be sceptical about the self-help books and neoliberal ideas of fixing midlife individually (discussed in Chapter 2), since care, duty and gender relations in midlife create plural and also constraining contexts for geographic moves such as that discussed here. Further, the example invites us to take a nuanced look at temporal horizons during the lifecourse (Lulle 2014; Amrith 2022). In the process of being in midlife, while future ageing contributes to important decisions about what to do and where to live, the past – in this example, lived in a place where one does not feel that one belongs – matters too, as does the capacity to aspire to a different life, not only for the future but also now (Robinson and Moen 2000; Bhat et al 2022).

Home in late midlife

In some final vignettes about home, I contrast experiences of the inherited home with instability due to tenancy or relationship issues. Inheritance is a typical event for many people in midlife. However, there are stark differences in what people inherit, and having a new or second home can change people's social and spatial positioning. In contrast, rather little is known about housing tenure and how it influences home-making practices (though one example is Bate 2018), let alone about the relationship between housing tenure and midlife. Let us turn to some examples that offer insight into these aspects.

Uldis, who I introduced in Chapter 3, inherited a large country house close to a busy regional city when he was 50. The house had belonged to his second wife's parents. Uldis and his wife had a happy marriage, so they treated the inheritance as 'ours', not the wife's. Around that time, he left his busy, stressful job, and the couple sold a post-Soviet-style flat in the city and began renovating the country property, which had a floor-space of around 200 square metres. The couple was not rich, either by Western European standards or by Latvian or other Eastern European standards, where inheriting a country house, even one with a large floor-space and relatively close to a city, can come either as a blessing or a curse. I heard black-and-white judgements on this type of property very often among midlifers. The key was whether the heirs had money, courage, contacts with builders and renovators, time and the willingness to move into the old house or keep it as a second property.

Houses, like humans, also have a lifecourse with historical period, place, timing and perhaps even material agency that interacts with human lifecourses. In Uldis' case, I propose that the inherited house changed his lifecourse: he left his job, worked on the house, then went to work abroad to generate income to put towards the renovation, and during our last interview looked back on his midlife from the age of 50 to his early sixties as a time of great growth, learning, diverse work and meaningful relationships (Moen 2003). The couple wanted to keep as much historical detail and structure as they could in their log house, which had been built in the 19th century. However, when the renovation work began, it turned out that the foundations were rotten to the extent that it was not possible to repair them. Uldis, through connections from his previous public sector job, contacted the best renovators (according to his judgement) in the country, who arrived with all the necessary technologies, pulled the house off its foundations, built new ones and then renovated the rest of the house. When all that was done, the renovated building was placed onto the new foundations. To some extent, more than a decade of Uldis' midlife resembled the lifecourse of his house: he pulled himself out of his foundation-like job, which no longer served the needs of his mind and body, learned new jobs, lived in different countries and returned home just before retirement, renewed and with a broader worldview.

Laila, a Latvian woman in her mid-fifties, also lived in a private house inherited by her husband from his parents. She was one of my key research participants during 2022–2023, and she allowed me to observe her daily life over many days, during which time I made a broad range of observations, complemented by multiple conversations with Laila. She and her husband had slowly grown apart over the years. Her husband was working in the UK and in Nordic countries, undertaking jobs that allowed him to be home in Latvia for long periods and then spend a few months abroad, earning money. Through his travels, he developed an independent lifestyle, and he began to nag Laila, saying that the house actually belonged to him. But Laila lived in the house and also worked from home for almost 30 years during their marriage. Home is very complex dynamic that can create the very basis of ontological security; equally, it can be an oppressive space and place that constraints agency (Blunt and Dowling 2006). The midlife home, seen through the lenses of home materiality and relationships, is a jewel for social and cultural geographers that awaits appreciation. Instability in relationships can last for many years, and not everyone makes the decision to separate. In fact, in my research, many of the middle-aged people whose relationships had ended, had rather reorganized their homes to accommodate separate living in midlife and still lived under the same roof as their ex-partner. But insecurity is greatest for those, often women, who are not officially the owners of properties bought or inherited prior to marriage or a long-term relationship.

Insecurity of tenancy is especially well-known to those middle-aged migrants who cannot afford to buy or take out a mortgage on a property. Ilze, a Latvian woman in her late fifties at the time of our last conversations, had moved to Finland during her forties after her previous relationship ended, and found a new partner. The new couple worked well together, but neither of them had enough income or stability to purchase a flat in their forties. Ilze was unemployed, or underemployed, most of the time, while her partner undertook some stints of intellectual work which were short term and project based. Hence, they always rented, not because they wanted to but because they never had enough savings for a deposit or future prospects for safe, permanent jobs. Housing insecurities such as this have important consequences for psychosocial wellbeing (Clarke and Kearns 2012; Baker et al 2013).

Jumping from one part-time job to another, Ilze's wellbeing deteriorated and she suffered health issues that were exacerbated by the insecurity of uncertain accommodation. During my last interview with her, she already knew that the owner of the flat they lived in wanted to sell within the next six months.

> It is hard ... to search again for a new space. We have books and all the things. It is not that we can simply move somewhere, to a one-room flat. In the meantime, we need to keep this flat open and presentable to possible buyers who come for house-viewing.

These are the mundane chores that make up ontological insecurity in midlife. Ilze ruled out a move back to Latvia; there was no opportunity for her to own property there, so the couple would be tenants again, and there would be limited work opportunities for her partner. Despite their insecure housing situation, she was happy with the good relationship she had with her partner. The realities of housing and tenancy insecurity described here should not be overlooked in future research. Next, I turn to cases that highlight the lens of linked lives in midlife.

Relationships in midlife

Relationships are the central theme in midlife. Relationships are usually complex and span several generations and extended families. In many cases, midlife relationships are ruptured, ties are severed, but some ties are renewed again.

Moving away from a ruptured family

I interviewed Ilze several times in Finland and Latvia, when she was in her early to mid-50s. She had a master's degree in business studies and several diplomas; she had one child and had moved to Finland in her late forties. Explaining why she emigrated from Latvia to Finland in the early 2010s, she told me: 'My family fell apart.' One day, after almost two decades together, Ilze's husband announced that he was bored romantically and wanted an open relationship (cf the concept of 'liquid love' in Bauman 2001; see also Giddens 1991 on changing intimacy in modern societies). Ilze refused: 'It was not acceptable to me.'

When Ilze decided to migrate, both Finland and Latvia were EU countries, so the borders were open. Nevertheless, job-seeking was difficult, despite her master's degree and diverse skills (see also Pöllänen and Davydova 2017 on middle-aged migrant women's structural precarity in the Finnish job market). Some help came from her new partner's academic acquaintances (that is, weak ties), but most were (like her) foreigners and on temporary contracts. Finally, an acquaintance suggested a part-time job at a start-up company. The job brought the security she needed to care for her growing son. She needed to remain in Finland and be employed to guarantee a study loan for her son, who was about to go to a university in another country. Thus, she was not free to move to another country for work, even though she had job offers abroad. In the meantime, her partner grew critical of her son, which caused tensions. Ilze told me: 'I left him because my son is the top priority.' She looked for a partner who would be her equal and would not criticize her ties with her son. During this time, she lived on a basic income and social benefits.

Ilze found that new friendships were difficult to establish. She had some acquaintances from the former Soviet Union and people she knew through her child's school – that is, horizontal weak ties. However, her most important social circle comprised Latvian acquaintances from organized meet-ups, events and cultural activities supported by the Latvian embassy in Finland – again, these were weak horizontal ties, but they were enabled by vertical ties to acquaintances in more resourceful positions who were able to organize such events and activities. Ilze said: 'They are good people, but they are acquaintances … not close friends. For several years, I was going back to Latvia for longer weekends almost every month, my closest people are there.' When she returned to Latvia, strong ties – her aunt and her former husband – were crucial for the practical arrangements. Ilze stayed in her aunt's apartment and in her ex-husband's apartment when she travelled to Latvia alone. When she described 'travelling alone', she paused and we both understood the subtext related to societal stereotypes and potential scorn for those who sever strong ties through migration. As women, we shared insights on how we, as women, repair such ties and how, as migrants, we need to arrange visits to our home countries on limited budgets.

Ilze became proficient in Finnish and spent two years studying for a new profession. Her son graduated, but Ilze's job security was volatile. She bounced from one project to another;

as she put it: 'Like a frog in a tub of cream, I keep kicking and churning.' She went to many networking events for people who had migrated from overseas and sought opportunities to secure her next job. Attending these networking events – which often took place in the evenings or at the weekend, or even as retreats with overnight stays – was only possible because she did not have hands-on care duties. Extant theories would consider her 'yo-yo' transitions to be a deviation from the standard transition from school to stable work (Du Bois-Reymond and López Blasco 2003). She was highly educated, hardworking and energetic, but her work was precarious (similar to the position many young professionals are in) due to the type of project-related, part-time jobs she had in Finland. Yet, she cared for her adult child and renewed links with her ex-husband and his new family to facilitate her regular transnational returns.

A second example involves Daiga, a Latvian woman who moved to Finland two decades ago. While Ilze and Daiga shared similar demographic characteristics (they were both divorced with teenage children), their macro-social contexts were very different. Daiga had a secondary and vocational education and left her teenage child behind in Latvia when she moved. She was 59 when I interviewed her in Finland. Daiga assumed it would be better if her son – still a young teenager – stayed in Latvia with her ex-husband. This was before Latvia joined the EU. Daiga ruptured her strong ties and care routines in Latvia but built new strong ties with her husband (at least formally). As soon as Daiga started learning Finnish and received integration support from the Finnish state, she realized that she had married a stranger with whom she had nothing in common apart from a sports hobby. Daiga divorced him as soon as she could.

These sorts of experiences with midlife migration call established divisions between strong and weak ties into question. Daiga found an internship (in her forties) through the Finnish integration programme, which led to a stable job. Her emancipation was made possible through information, which flowed from both horizontal and vertical weak ties – work colleagues and new bosses. 'I then immediately joined a trade union and realized how much support and protection is available from the state', she recalled. Thus, state structures not social networks, led to a better life for Daiga. Fortunately, her son did not hold negative feelings towards her for leaving him with his father, and after he studied abroad he found a good job. Daiga described how, despite the loss of her strong ties in Latvia, she was able to develop friendship ties with her son:

> I blamed myself. It was my life's biggest tragedy that I separated from him. But he has never blamed me. We now travel together around the world, and I live in his house [on a different continent] for several months. Not many parents become so close to their adult children.

These stories capture the nature of relationships in midlife. Ilze was jumping from one precarious job to other, but she maintained strong ties with her new partner and her son and even renewed acquaintance-type relations with her ex-husband. Daiga's midlife story depicts her revival after rupturing of strong ties, a path she attributes to her inner drive for self-actualization. After long periods of guilt at having left her child behind, she was able to reconnect with her (adult) son later on.

Extended family ties for migration and return

In some final stories about relationships, I offer male perspectives on migration in midlife. The first story involves Edgars, who had qualifications in woodwork and was working as carpenter and in construction in Latvia. He was not married and was in his late thirties when he left for the UK, together with some former colleagues from various construction projects he had worked on (that is, horizontal weak ties). However, there had been another important episode in his life prior to this, related to his extended family – that is, his strong ties in Latvia (he only realized the significance of this episode when he was 50 and decided to return to Latvia). His father had passed away when he was a young boy, and his mother died when he was in his thirties. According to law, he was one of the heirs of the parental house. However, since the house, in a remote small town in Latvia, was in poor condition and required significant renovations, Edgars had not been eager to take on this burden. In addition, his siblings and aunts had persuaded him to give up his inheritance rights as he was leaving for the UK anyway and would not be available to take care of the cumbersome paperwork related to the house.

Edgars forgot about the house for a good decade, during which time he worked in the UK and had intermittent spells of work in Spain. Workwise, his community, while changing from time to time, consisted mainly of several former construction work colleagues from Latvia (weak horizontal ties). The opportunities to work in Spain were facilitated by new weak vertical ties – Latvian and British bosses who had construction-related business there.

Edgars got married during this time. In his forties, he met a Latvian woman, younger than him. She was also working in the UK, though after becoming pregnant, she followed Edgars to Spain; when the child was born, she became a stay-at-home mother, and she continued this role when the family returned to the UK. When their child was approaching school age, the couple came to the decision to return to Latvia. Edgars explained:

> [The child] was speaking fluent English. She understood Latvian but often preferred to answer in English. We then were seriously thinking: 'Who are we? We are not British but our child soon will not be Latvian either.' Then we made the decision to return … I knew from acquaintances that I wouldn't have difficulties finding a job.

Indeed, on returning to the capital city of Riga, Edgars quickly picked up several woodwork projects from previous ties with construction colleagues. However, at this time, he realized that not only had he become estranged from his extended family, but he had also lost out financially, since the parental house had been renovated and sold for good money – he realized he could have used his share of profits as starting funds to buy a property for his own family. In sum, Edgars' story, while it is about returning to his home country, is also a story of ruptured ties with an extended family and of the social agency his own nuclear family demonstrated in making decisions about their life together.

In contrast, Arvids, a married father of four and highly educated, left Latvia at the age of 49 for an unskilled job in a food processing factory in the UK. His wife remained in Latvia as she had a stable administrative job and their youngest child was still in the early teens. Arvids' main motivation for the move was to earn a higher income – an unskilled job in the UK offered around three times the income he made in Latvia. He returned to Latvia only twice a year and gradually became estranged from his wife. The main link between the couple was the constant flow of remittances from Arvids to his wife and their youngest child.

However, on one of his return visits, the couple visited the wife's father, who was frail and living alone in a country house. His wife did not want to provide care, as it would require her to give up her job for an unknown period, but a care home (in short supply in Latvia at the time) was not an option as the man did not want to leave his house. It was Arvids who decided to stay and care for his father-in-law, in spite of the fact he and his wife were already partially estranged. Here, the strong ties of the extended family were evident. Arvids was not worried about losing his job in the UK; there were always jobs in the factory, he said. His living arrangements in the UK were not a problem either, as he rented a house with two of his cousins, and it was possible to take in a tenant on a temporary basis, which would mean there would be a place for Arvids to live whenever he wanted to come back. He cared for his father-in-law for half a year, until the man's final days, and then he went back to work in the UK so that he could qualify for the state pension.

When I last interviewed Arvids, he was newly retired according to Latvian legislation, though he still needed to work for several years in the UK before he would receive the state pension. His plan for after that was to return to Latvia for good, though not to his family. He wanted to live alone as long as possible, health permitting.

Conclusion

In this chapter, I looked at midlife geographies and lifecourses through the vantage points of home and relationships. This adds to the exploration of midlife transitions related to body and work in Chapter 3. These four perspectives together – though not an exhaustive list of the lenses that can best illuminate the complexity of social and spatial arrangements in midlife – form a foundation for understanding the intertwined layers of midlife temporalities and spatialities. I propose that we can productively use the concept of transitions in terms of body and, to some extent, work, where the institutional ideas of linear transitions remain persistently hegemonic (Potter 2020). However, in terms of home and relationships, it is more useful to see these concepts as processes in midlife.

Home is a scale and lens par excellence in midlife geographies. It entails such richness of generational places and histories, in terms of both materialities and values. As institutional ideals and perceptions of how middle-aged people should live and what kind of home arrangements they should have are, and have been, hegemonic in society, home is a realm where we can further advance understanding of economic and political temporalities and timing in lifecourses. Recentring research on home in midlife studies will help us to challenge Whiteness and middle-class patriarchal relations which underpin older theories of lifecourse. The widespread midlife insecurities about home, such as precarious work, potentially contribute to poorer ageing (Robinson and Moen 2000; Grenier et al 2020). This was certainly so in the Latvian and Latvian-related cases I studied. Unscrutinized assumptions of stability not only negatively affect people's lives but also prevent them from seeing and understanding the plurality of lived lives and how people in middle age produce spaces (Hörschelmann 2011). Hence, I want to add to the current definitions of lifecourse – which take account of time, place, timing and linked lives (cf Elder 1994) – the materiality of home as a fundamental element in understanding lifecourse, not only locally but also through transnational temporal and spatial scales.

In terms of relationships, I moved away from the trivialized (though it is actually not trivial) notion of midlife transition as a crisis. Instead, I demonstrated that midlife is a process filled with myriad intra-generational, intergenerational and networked relations that are prone to ruptures, but which also have distinct continuities and potential for revival. More needs to be done to show how the youth transition of establishing one's own home happens and how it is vitally shaped and produced through relationships in midlife. I provided an insight into how early midlifers capitalize on the positive notion of the 'young family' to mobilize moral duties and solidarity among relatives and acquaintances. The quality and type of relationship are specifically reconfigured in midlife. Hence, I invite future researchers to look more closely at networks and linked lives in midlife. While we know that family connections (strong ties) are crucial in the linked lives and spatial dynamics of lifecourses (Carr 2018), I also demonstrated how the specific generational experience of transition from socialism and post-socialism to neoliberal capitalism in midlife shapes values and relationships. A focus on midlife reveals that the strong ties of family and close friends stretch across the longer lifecourse and morph into weak ties or that they are severed and renewed in specific ways, which are distinct from youth and older age lifecourses.

FIVE

Geographies of Menopausing

Introduction

A menopause 'revolution' is happening. In the UK, people are marching in parks, signing petitions, demonstrating outside Parliament and demanding education, care and work policies for all who are experiencing menopause symptoms (Menopause Mandate nd). In the Nordic country of Finland, new books and films on the subject are frequently released and digital sites are booming with 'sisterhood' support (Edwards et al 2021). In Latvia, menopause appears in the media more often, though almost exclusively with expert knowledge provided by medical doctors. These activities point towards varied geographies of increased awareness on this crucial gendered process, which is spatially distinct. While the extant medicalized approach acknowledges large geographical differences in symptom experience, it typically does not consider the social process of this human condition. What we are witnessing in the 2020s is people demanding that experts recognize and value their lived experiences.

In this chapter, I argue that the diversity lens and geography are fundamental in seeking answers to social change around menopause awareness. Moreover, not only does menopause affect more than half the population, but it involves myriad human and more-than-human interconnections. Nor is it a one-off event; menopausing, an apt term used by McCall and Potter (2022), is a temporal, spatial and, of course, sharply gendered process that stretches over decades in midlife and beyond. Amini and McCormack (2019) refer to it as 'menopausal time', a process rather than a singular biological event. These ways of seeing serve as a departure point to decipher temporalities of menopause. And there is more. The long process of menopausing, which is one of the most divisive, stereotyped, scary yet potentially empowering and place- and culture-specific personal processes, operates within historical and contemporary power relations of ageism and patriarchy. It needs to be addressed as historical oppression, showing women's place in the world (Domosh and Seager 2001). But before making arguments for diversity, awareness of multiplicity and activism, I unpack the contexts that have led to patriarchal and ageist views of this important process. The chapter therefore builds on temporal, spatial and scalar takes on social change. From global to national and local scales, I scrutinize how awareness and demands can lead to change in practices and policies in concrete spaces and relations, and I propose future avenues for research that have the potential to shift broader theoretical understandings of gender and ageing over time and space.

How have these recent shifts, especially those in the UK, occurred, and why does it matter? In the recent examples of activism, menopause awareness almost always advances from a personal experience of shame and fear on a bodily scale. As I demonstrated in Chapter 2, on midlife narratives, because of the ways women's experiences have been silenced and siloed in the realms of the sicker sex and ageism, it comes as no surprise that menopause awareness is such hard work even today. It is common that these experiences are post factum, told as a struggle in silence and secrecy over extended periods. Many resourceful activists – politicians, famous journalists and activist gynaecologists – when they received help or found solutions (hormone treatments and other solutions) that restored some normalcy in their life, decided to break their silence (Forstrup and Smellie 2021). To tell their very personal menopause stories, these activists created alliances with doctors and made reference to the work of gynaecological associations or other official guidelines as well as (often selectively and partially) medical scientific research that is national or global in scale. Such a mobilization of experts gives legitimacy to their claims (see Gunter 2021 on political efforts to recognize menopause as a significant issue for wellbeing and gender equality in the US, and Hackling and Mander 2022 on political visions and a taskforce assigned the job of changing menopause-related legislation in the UK).

However, there is an evident contradiction embedded in the context of menopause activism: menopause is described as 'natural event' and 'not a disease', although the symptoms must be explained by doctors and are pathologized. The treatment of symptoms is usually highly regulated. People become patients, dependent on visits to doctors and subject to disruptions in global supply chains of hormone treatment, or to use the common but potentially misleading pharmaceutical term, 'hormone replacement therapy' (or HRT) products. Further, activists – journalists, political figures and doctors working in the private sector – make an effort to emphasize that hormone treatment is a choice and that not all want this treatment (though in the latter case, this is often due to the now largely discredited fear that hormone therapy can cause cancer).

At the same time, activism for menopausing 'naturally' is widely popular and varied. Comparatively, only 10 to 14 per cent of menopausal people in the UK use hormone treatment. Well-known research on hormone treatment with one type of oestrogen, derived from mare urine, took place a generation ago. However, significantly, the International Women's Initiative, which organized the research, abruptly interrupted the study in 2002. Much medical research has followed, and medicines have changed, but media headlines saying that women who use hormones die from cancer, heart attack and stroke still have a real and frightening impact on people's lives (see Brown 2012).

Simultaneously, deep social, cultural, financial and racial inequalities became visible in sharp relief. Very few voices from ethnically and racially diverse communities are part of expert guidelines and medical research. So far, of the three countries I follow closely, only activists in the UK have realized this gap. Queer, Black and surgical menopause-experiencing people are raising their voices in awareness activism and arguing for multiple other pathways to bodily integrity (Glyde 2021; 2022). In sum, menopause, which is still unevenly stigmatized and silenced in some cultural milieus, continues to revolve around oppressive contradictions: it happens to more than half the world's population, yet few medical experts claim knowledge of it. Historically and in everyday life today, discourses and silences around menopause are prone to highly divisive interpretations, which can involve scaremongering and disinformation about women and their 'natural' and 'medicalized' ways of life. At the same time, the commercial supplements industry has cashed in on a grand scale, selling 'natural' remedies for anxious bodies. However, very little is known about the economic and environmental geographies of menopause, including how global supply chains operate, from raw materials to products reaching human bodies.

Inherent contradictions in the medical concept of menopause

Medical research has recognized that geography is a vital aspect of menopause; place and lifecourses matter to a great extent, but medical researchers do not have tools to approach these factors for the greater good of 'patients' (Palacious et al 2010; De Mello et al 2021). Therefore, medical researchers call on social researchers to develop social approaches to menopause research, as the gaps in social understanding decrease the capacity of medical approaches to address symptoms (see Schoenaker et al 2014). This is somewhat contradictory, as geographical and broader social research becomes a kind of servant addition to the master narrative of medical menopause.

An epistemological problem persists in the current way of theorizing menopause: largely, the current social research reproduces the contradiction embedded in the invention of the concept of menopause by French medical doctors (Moore 2022). This conceptual work took place during the French Revolution and its aftermath and led to profound changes in how spaces and people are organized in Western capitalist modernity. The conceptualization arising out of this work reflects the power of both the patriarchy and ageism. Menopause was defined as natural and inevitable for female bodies in midlife. The attention from the medical world is positive in the sense that it is a form of care. However, simultaneously, menopause was defined as sickness which requires treatment, paving the way for certain operations in female bodies and giving rise to the discipline of psychiatry (Moore 2022). Although the female population live longer (female mortality rates are lower than male mortality rates), it was defined as the more morbid (that is, sicker) sex, forming a large clientele for doctors and pharmacists. The outcome, psychosocially, was a concerned turning inwards, a worrying about ill-being gendered bodies instead of living outwards and claiming male-dominated space. Simultaneously, the concept denigrated women's self and folk knowledge related to menopausing (Moore 2022). Geographical and social differences added further layers to this concept, framing lazy elite urban dwellers as those who suffer most compared to rustic, hardworking countrywomen. This seminal analysis of the historical concept is our departure point. Further deconstruction of how people experience symptoms in certain countries can yield only limited case studies.

The lack of geographic contributions to menopause and midlife transitions can be attributed to the masculine and imperial origins of geography as a discipline (Hopkins and Pain 2007; DeLyser and Shaw 2013). However, bright and courageous feminist geographers irreversibly turned the tide in the 20th century (Monk and Hanson 1982). Hence, there is no excuse for excluding a large-scale gendered experience from the scrutiny of their sociospatiality. Moreover, going against the grain of established (medical) narratives opens up a rich field of study of gender and age geographies, which can inform the politics, resistance and transformation of places and social relations that make up spaces and places (Gambaudo 2017). While it has been overlooked and just scarcely mentioned in ageing, health or feminist geographies, social research has gained traction in the past decade – see, for example, work on menopause as a taboo and commercialization process (Grandey et al 2020; Krajewski 2018). There are several case studies of menopause geographies among specific groups of workers, such as the police (Atkinson et al 2021), women in executive positions (Carter et al 2021), physiotherapists (O'Hearn 2022), women in low-paid jobs (Verburgh et al 2020) and ambulance workers in the UK (Prothero et al 2021), and work on workplace policies (Geukes et al 2012; Atkinson et al 2015; Rees et al 2019; Atkinson et al 2021) as well as broader post-structural feminist approaches to women's needs and health priorities (Alspaugh et al 2021). This points towards the reality of a multiplicity of lived experiences that need to be, as DeLyser and Shaw (2013: 505) aptly put it, 'exhumated' from the departmentalism of knowledge and omission.

Working across siloes

Prior to any further proposition on a geographical approach to menopausing, several significant challenges – including medicalized language, work across disciplines and data gathering approaches – need to be explained. Medicalized language itself is a crucial challenge. We need to dig through quite a lot of wording and discourses that put women in their place, silencing them or encouraging them to change their lifestyle and make appointments with various doctors. Reading through these texts, I seek the language that foregrounds standpoints of lived experience and can start building resistance to hegemonic patriarchy and gendered ageism.

The second, and related, challenge is interdisciplinary work. Distressing symptoms are broadly documented in medicine. Meanwhile, anthropological studies have shown that menopause is shaped by culture (Lock 1993). Extant lifecourse literature emphasizes care, health and changes in personal relations in midlife (Lachman 2001; Moen 2003; Barrett 2005; Mahler 2011; MIDUS nd), but remains largely silent about the crucial transformations that menopausing brings to female and non-binary bodies, partners and work colleagues as well as children and ailing parents, for whom many menopausing people provide care. Wonderful geographies on how middle-aged women internally migrate, giving up their careers to care for their parents (Stockdale et al 2013), have similarly omitted issues around menopause. However, these literatures provide some building blocks to theorize menopausing, since care, health and personal relationships intertwine with menopausing.

The third challenge is to break away from the taken-for-granted approaches in data gathering that overlook existing diversity and social boundaries among menopausal people. In extant literature, it is typical to refer to statistics such as average age when menopause begins (albeit awkwardly, and diagnosed only retrospectively). Perimenopause is usually thought to emerge around the age of 40 or so, leading to a cessation of menstruation – again, in average terms, and assuming no previous surgery on the uterus or ovaries – around the early fifties. Lived experiences challenge assumptions that cessation of menses is merely a biological non-event, which ends in some years after the body has adjusted to reduced oestrogen. Such national averaging and symptom gathering within national boundaries are the default approach, flattening out inherent individual differences and lived experience even among culturally relatively homogeneous groups, let alone across today's transnational world.

Therefore, in this chapter I look at menopausing through the lens of temporalities and how geography matters in illuminating these temporary processes. Further, I look at the spatiality of menopausing in current literature and shed light on some of the (so far) less studied power processes of multibillion-dollar hormone therapy supply chains.

Individualized and averaged timing and temporalities

Translating signs rather than 'symptoms' through the lens of timing and temporality in the language women themselves prefer and, potentially, enrich through interpretation of scientific knowledge is a complex task. Perimenopause, menopause, and postmenopause can evoke paralysing affects that are challenging in different cultures. The medical term 'menopause' is defined post factum. It is assumed that menses stops for good around age 50 (for women who have not previously gone through a surgical menopause). When menses stop, doctors declare menopause after 12 months. Menopause, therefore becomes a somehow illusive moment that has already happened but can be announced only with a year's delay, when menopausing people are medically 'packaged' into the 'postmenopausal' group.

This is quite a contrast to lived experience. Often, periods become irregular long before they stop. And they can restart again during the hormonal changes leading to menopause. Such identification of a pause in pre-, peri- and postmenopause using the last menses post factum with a timing of 12 months is of little help, because, as most menopausal people have experienced, menstrual bleeding can be very messy and re-emerge. However, sticking to such flawed timings has a real and detrimental consequence in people's lives (see Menopause Mandate nd). By sticking to existing top-down timing practices (where an expert decides the stage a person is at), some are denied menopause treatment because they are too young and do not fit the average age of onset (taking the countries I have studied most, this average age is 51 in Finland and the UK and 52 in Latvia) or too old, as the symptoms should have already have finished.

In medical literature, the lengthy process of menopausing, which encompasses peri-, pre- and postmenopause, is typically defined as the time between the ages of 40 and 65. Medically, menopause is often portrayed as a natural biological phenomenon marking the cessation of reproductive capacity in females; however, it is a multifaceted and culturally contingent process. Its manifestation and impact vary significantly across temporal, geographic and sociocultural contexts, reflecting a complex interplay of biological, psychological and social factors (DeLyser and Shaw 2013). Medically, the temporal dimension tends to narrate the experience of menopause as a distinct phase of life, with potentially longer durations and more pronounced symptoms. Scientific knowledge in the medical field links these cultural and geographic influences to individual variations in genetics, hormone profiles and overall health status, further contributing to the diversity of menopause experiences.

Historically, in terms of the age when menopause begins, Flint (1976) marked out only one geographic factor. According to this historical study, altitude has been found to accelerate female hormonal ageing. No socioeconomic factors have been conclusively discussed in other historical studies from the 20th century (Leuf 1902, cited in Flint 1997). A recent study of the history and geography of menopause age and space dynamics in Portugal (Martins et al 2022) demonstrated that from the early 20th century up to the 1960s, the typical menopause age increased by 2.49 years (from 47.10 years in 1910 to 49.59 years in 1960), with regional differences. The increase was attributed to social geography, rather than physical geography, factors: menopause tends to come earlier in poorer regions. A study of nine European countries between 1998 and 2002 demonstrated that cessation of menses is strongly linked to chronological age – that is, around the early fifties (Dratva et al 2009). A quarter of the women in this study were postmenopausal by age 50.8 years. The median age of natural menopause was 54 years. However, the study also admitted that age at menopause varies across Europe and is shifting upwards. Other studies confirm this chronological age marker. Palacios et al (2010) found that the median age at menopause in Europe ranges from 50.1 to 52.8 years, in North America from 50.5 to 51.4 years, in Latin America from 43.8 to 53 years, and in Asia from 42.1 to 49.5 years (see also similar results by Schoenaker et al 2014).

In both Asia and Latin America, women of poorer socioeconomic status have significantly earlier menopause Palacios et al (2010). This data points towards social, cultural and spatial contexts that, so far, are poorly understood. In addition, the persistent hegemonic narrative of menopause as an event that marks not only biological ageing but also chronic ill health in later life creates further challenges for social researchers trying to excavate meaningful and life-affirming practices for middle-aged people who are going through menopause and simultaneously have decades of working life ahead of them in our rapidly ageing world.

Intergenerational times of silencing

More than two decades ago, an important science communication event happened in what we can call the intergenerational time (cf Giddens 1984) of structuring the medical and patriarchal management, and treatment, of menopause. A large-scale study of hormone therapy for menopausal women (it was still time when non-binary and queer gender was not recognized) was abruptly interrupted after an interim evaluation. This study, by the Women's Health Initiative in the US, used one type of hormone therapy, oral tablets called Premarin, for which oestrogen was derived from pregnant mares. Sparing the reader the multiple contexts leading to this interruption, the key scare factor relates to the study's 'one size fits all' approach – that is, giving one type of therapy to all women, regardless of their age, underlying health conditions and lifestyles. Thereafter, (mis)interpreting the data, media headlines warned that women who use hormone therapy were at risk of early death, cancer, strokes and more (Brown 2012).

The important thing here is to understand what has happened between this study and now. Trémollieres et al (2022) claim that a persistent gap in menopause care emerged for a whole generation of menopausal people. Unlike the situation before the study, after the study was interrupted, most women across many Western countries feared using hormone treatment. I got a sense of the aftermath of this particular study in my research on ageing in Latvia, far from the US. In my study, carried out during 2022–2023, women in their seventies remembered well how they were 'bombarded' with offers to use hormones in their fifties, and their stories tell of how they avoided these offers. Looking back on their lives, how they avoided taking hormones was usually presented to me as a strength and a demonstration of intuitive wisdom. This was a retrospective argument in the light of scaremongering from the interrupted study far from Latvia. The greatest repercussion for the next generation, which was entering menopause across different countries, was that they kept silent about symptoms that influence quality of life: excessive tiredness, muscle and joint pain, and much more beyond stereotypical symptoms such as hot flashes. Multiple studies confirmed this silence. For example, Nappi et al (2023) found that 44 per cent of more than five thousand women surveyed in Western countries never discussed their symptoms with doctors, 62 per cent said they had decided not to use hormone treatment and that this decision was supported by their doctors, and only 6 per cent were taking hormone treatment.

Perceptions and cultural attitudes vary by country, and particularly by class (because highly skilled and economically well-off menopausal people tend to use hormone therapy more than poorer people), but the fear of death from hormone treatment seems persist. With many studies in the medical literature over the past decades suffering from different methodological and potential gendered bias, menopause signs are portrayed so differently that any building on these generalized symptomological foundations would be very shaky. The newest studies, however, tend to suggest that very high numbers of people do experience symptoms. For example, Panay et al (2021) found that around 90 to 97 per cent of Europeans and Australians experienced physical symptoms, with the UK leading the ranks of symptom experience; only 8 per cent of Europeans reported no physical or psychological symptoms during menopausing.

Class, race and ethnicity have become prominent categories in studies of menopause. Much research reveals how racialized menopause neglect is (for example, Aririguzo et al 2022 in the US and Makuwa et al 2015 in South Africa), with a lack of knowledge of cultural differences and a lack of dignity for women. Avis et al (2001), using data from 14,906 women in the US, conclude that White women are more concerned with psychological and psychosomatic symptoms, while African American women are more bothered by vasomotor symptoms, such as hot flashes. While this and similar studies carried out two decades ago to some extent demonstrate that intersections of race and gender are important, they do not explain why. In another study, Delanoë et al (2012: 401), in a somewhat sweeping comparative manner, conclude that among Tunisian women in Tunisia, Tunisian women in France, and French women in France, all aged from 45 to 70, Tunisian working-class women in Tunisia and France experience menopause with the most intense symptoms and have a stronger sense of 'social degradation'. Further divisions along class and race-ethnicity lines in this study show that Tunisian middle-class women, both in France and Tunisia, are more concerned with social and aesthetic factors than physical symptoms, while French women see little or no change in their social value. The point the authors rightly make is that differences are not biological but social (see also Ferrand et al 2013). The economic situation, but most importantly the grip of patriarchy and ageism, play the major role in how menopausing times are lived through. We can see this even more dramatically in Iran, where menopause is perceived as a serious sickness (Amini and McCormack 2019; Amini 2023).

However, these studies go beyond assumptions of social loss, albeit this is a central narrative for Iranian women. Importantly, these studies are at pains to elicit how women, in the given patriarchal and religious contexts, use body regimes and resistance in their own ways to negotiate sexual activity and reject social expectations. They build non-Western epistemologies, referring to agency as rooted less in traditional forms of free will and more in tactical negotiations in the given contexts (Bassel 2012). While menopause is experienced as more traumatic and different from menopause in Western societies, where the room for manoeuvre in gender freedom is larger, not agreeing to sexual activities that are painful and unwanted can be understood as feminist activism (Amini and McCormack 2019). Research itself in strict patriarchal and religious contexts provides space for participants to reflect and contribute towards a wider agenda of raising awareness.

Neuroculture and putting women in their place

Today, what women fear most about menopause are changes in memory and cognitive symptoms, at least according to the booming awareness spaces in digital environments. Why is this so? I argue that the neoliberal culture of achievement and successful ageing and the constant pressure to have a sharp and productive mind is at play here, because people worry about mental rather than physical ailments in encounters with ageing. Medical studies from decades ago have entrenched a discourse that people in midlife show a steady decline in memory performance (see, for example, Lavigne and Finley 1990).

This fear of 'losing one's mind' and showing early signs of dementia are widespread among menopausing people, beginning early with perimenopause hormonal fluctuations. Tiredness due to multiple care pressures, workload and, most importantly, poor sleep massively contribute to mental ill-being during the long years of menopausing (Bellipanni et al 2005; McCarthy and Raval 2020). These symptoms also exacerbate the fear of ageing in poor health, but more acutely can bring a paralysing fear of job loss due to an inability to remember words or perform tasks as quickly as before. McCall and Potter (2022), Forstrup and Smellie (2021) and Newson (2023) give vivid illustrations of and autobiographical insights into how terrifying the fear of not remembering words can be. In the era of active and successful ageing ideologies, demands on people in middle age can be overwhelming. Along with established divisions between 'third' and 'fourth' types of old age, the former meaning healthy and active people and the latter frail, non-working people in need of care (Williams 2012; Higgs and Gilleard 2017), neurocultural pressures to perform best in midlife must be critically scrutinized. Activists, especially medical doctors advocating better hormone therapy, emphasize that mental health and memory issues are more important and more scary than hot flashes and demand more research and education for both doctors and broader society on how the brain works differently in ageing among females and males (Newson 2023).

This is why more serious and critical scrutiny of neurocultural pressures need to be on the agenda along with other menopausing issues. Research has shown that menopause can influence various aspects of mental wellbeing, including mood, cognitive function and risk of anxiety and depression. Along with other compounded issues of ageism and cultural stigmatization, it is difficult even to mention the word 'menopause' in many spaces across the world. People keep silent about how they feel and force themselves to work according to the same patriarchal and capitalist rules of performance and efficiency as they did in youth, when bodily energy levels were much higher and care duties usually minimal. This focus on energy levels undermines the considerable professional experience that people in midlife have. By valuing experience instead, it becomes clear that it would be even more productive for people in midlife to work less while still achieving good results (more on this in Chapter 6). This is to say nothing of the larger ethical issues of life satisfaction and collective efforts to resist exploitative capitalist practices.

What current mainstream agendas propose is to use hormone treatment, cognitive-behavioural therapy, mindfulness-based interventions and lifestyle modifications like exercise and dietary changes (National Institute for Health and Care Excellence 2023). Research across the globe keeps proposing mindfulness, self-compassion and acceptance of change (as is evident in Thailand – see Arpanantikul 2006 – and Japan – see Hashiguchi et al 2021). While these potentially benevolent propositions have benefits, they also hold the danger of playing into the agenda of the patriarchy: menopausing people need to change the ways they think, their 'wrong' thinking causes their problems, and so on. Such approaches individualize and usher into private spaces of counselling and treatment what is collective – that is, the dramatic hormonal changes that many go through – further entrenching existing trends of shaming (for example, fat shaming and body image obsession leads to eating disorders in midlife; see Midlarsky and Nitzburg 2008). In addition, psychosocial factors relating to menopause symptoms are linked to the flawed early biological portrayal of females as the sicker sex due to their biology (Binfa et al 2004). In 2023, UK menopause activists began raising their voices against this cognitive 'fixing' of menopausal bodies (see, for example, Muir 2023; Newson 2023).

These trends are in plain sight for geographers to embrace and analyse seriously. How are middle-aged people treated in the workplace compared to their younger colleagues and the pre-retirement group? How do midlifers claim space and time for their work, which supports their needs and those of their workplace and is not at the expense of an exhausted menopausal body? Nocturnal geographies would gain so much fresh insight if they would openly interrogate what it means to work a full shift after a sleepless night. I now turn, therefore, to an analysis of how menopausing matters in everyday spaces.

Everyday spaces

Workplaces, arguably, are to date the most studied space in relation to menopausing. However, far more research and data are needed on the work people do in diverse countries and cultures across the globe, be it physically demanding physiotherapy work (O'Hearn 2022), work that involves dealing with stressful events, such as in police workspaces (Atkinson et al 2021), work in a range of executive and public work spaces (see Carter et al's 2021 study in Australia and New Zealand), or the work of teaching staff (see Hammam et al's 2012 study in Egypt). We know some of the tactics women use to manage and tactically resist oppressive structures that ignore bodily needs, an example being leaving the room in the middle of a meeting to get through a hot flash (Butler 2020; see also de Certeau 1984 on tactics for use of spaces). Unsurprisingly, a dominant trend in the literature is patriarchal and masculine – it is about menopause as something that needs to be managed in the workplace because it causes a burden and has humanistic and economic implications (Dibonaventura et al 2013). The direction of much of this type of thinking is to reduce direct costs, either societal or (more importantly) business costs. In other words, fixing vasomotor symptoms is thought to fix people so that they can regain their previously productive working bodies.

However, other and more nuanced research demonstrates that such thinking is a broad oversimplification. Symptoms and ill-being are intersectional. Oppressed groups, especially along sexuality, class, ethnicity and race intersections, cannot be simply and quietly fixed without truly opening up uncomfortable questions of racism and exclusion and moving from individual tactics to strategic recognition of social difference as a fundamental issue of workplace policies (Jack et al 2019; 2021; Riach and Jack 2021; Steffan 2021). Making more washrooms, and making them more accessible, would benefit all, but more toilets, showers or fans for hot flashes will not fix ageism or sexism, which are deeply ingrained in many structures of today's workplaces. They can give wins for managerial culture when implementing diversity changes in the workplace. However, only a comprehensive wellbeing strategy for menopause, tackling the structural oppression of gendered ageing and racism, will do the real work (Targett and Beck 2022).

In terms of home spaces, geographers are at the forefront of the social sciences in demonstrating how home can be not only a cosy place for rest and recovery but also an oppressive and exhausting place (Blunt 2005; Brickell 2012). What happens behind the closed doors of home to menopausing people across the globe (see Bhakta 2018 on home experiences in Ghana) should be of high importance to feminist and social and cultural geographers. The massive commercialization, and advertising agenda, of nutrition pushes menopausing people to meditate (neuroculture again), calm down, make their spaces peaceful and quiet, and eat radically differently. How are these pressures reconciled with family needs, and how do they introduce new routines and relationships? We know from some research, such as Amini (2023) in Iran, that menopause exhaustion can serve as a stepping stone to resist patriarchal service as women simply lack the strength, or rather they must muster new strength, to say no to endless cooking and cleaning up after family members. Ultimately, by not taking up the job of scrutinizing the home places of menopausing people academically, researchers play into the status quo, the patriarchal agenda of silencing menopause behind closed doors.

Importantly, digital spaces have rapidly become a refuge, a support and an educative place for menopausing people. It is here, rather than in short visits to a medical doctor, that the most heated discussions take place and where many people learn much more about menopause and almost every other aspect of life that it influences. Digital spaces are arguably the most important platforms for the new wave of feminism of everyday life, where political claims are forged (Zimmerman 2017). Of the countries I follow closely, the UK is clearly leading with highly visible, loud and interconnected digital spaces on Instagram and other social media platforms, including the specially created spaces of Menopause Mandate. The LGBTQIA+ and non-binary experience of menopause has achieved a significantly strong presence globally through dedicated digital spaces and resources and alliances with other activists (Glyde 2021). Similarly, there is no excuse to say that we (either medical doctors or a wider White public) know little about Black menopause, as activists have created and interlinked a wealth of digital resources on lived experiences of diverse social groups.

National and transnational scales: politics and the economy of menopausing

Menopause, without doubt, is an issue of national and global importance when it comes to money. Therefore, I want to briefly shed light on themes that geographers across the subdisciplines can advance for better understanding of gendered human lives and care, and on how these are shaped by licencing and acquiring goods through menopause medicine supply chains. The geographical understanding of these supply chains requires a nuanced appreciation of spatial relationships, transportation dynamics, economic disparities and geopolitical factors. I want to emphasize the ethics of care for populations managed by governments (Rose 1993). Ultimately, businesses and policy makers alike must leverage this understanding to create robust and adaptive supply chain strategies that can serve the needs of menopausing people. When researching this book, I checked out how many types of oestrogen and other hormone products were available in the UK, which despite Brexit is still a core economy and consumer market in Europe and well connected to other core markets globally. I found that there were dozens of products of different kinds, such as patches, gels, sprays, tablets, pessaries and implants. The market for unlicenced, so-called bio-identical products, was booming in private boutique clinics, and these products were widely discussed in the UK and the US. A variety of products, albeit narrower in range, were also licenced in Finland. However, the choices in the economically weaker and significantly smaller consumer market in Latvia (a country of approximately 1.8 million inhabitants) were rather limited. Regulatory oversight exerts a substantial influence on the availability of hormone medicines. Pharmaceutical companies and governments can prioritize the production of certain medications over others, and if a hormone treatment is seen as something of a niche market, they go down the list of priority supply.

A big challenge is opacity and lack of information on how hormone products are created from raw materials to laboratory, and how they are supplied geographically, including to specific pharmacies and individual users. This secrecy of how products for menopausal people are prepared is at odds with other widely popular research on food geographies, including work on the conditions of those who grow crops and those who package and distribute them through geography's vital interests in transportation modes (for example, road, rail, sea, air), and work on the climate change-aware selection of transportation routes. What we know so far is rather journalistic – for example, we have fragmentary insights into the import of soya beans to make oestrogen products in European laboratories (Adu 2023). But menopausal people know nothing of the work conditions of growers or profit distribution along the supply chain. When I visited a doctor in Finland in 2023, one of the most important moments in our conversation was when she checked her phone to tell me where to find a pharmacy that had the product I needed. It turned out that across the map of Finland she consulted, orange dots indicated that more than 90 per cent of pharmacies were out of the product. It was only because of the lucky coincidence that I had planned a 400-kilometre trip to a remote town that week that I was able to get three months' supply there. We know equally little about the growing of yams, which are used for natural progesterone, albeit some earlier fragmentary research on the use of yams for other medicines, such as painkillers, indicates that serious geographies of extraction, inequality and exploitation of the Global South are waiting to be uncovered.

Healthcare policy and reimbursement mechanisms can also reveal how governments care for the wellbeing of their people when it comes to hormone treatment availability. Policies related to drug pricing, reimbursement rates and insurance coverage can influence the financial viability of manufacture and distribution of hormone medications and entrench inequalities between people. This is one of the central issues in the demands of menopause activists from the UK to Australia to the US (see, for example, Menopause Mandate nd). The welfare state in Finland, for instance, applies a 40 per cent discount to some oestrogen products, while other individually necessary hormone products, such as natural progesterone or (non-licenced or off-label in most countries) testosterone products, remain expensive and hence price-prohibiting for many users.

Institutional ethnographies and feminist economy studies of supply chains are yet to come, but research on production of space could potentially yield far-reaching results that aid understanding of the opaque and often secretive relationships between pharmaceutical manufacturers, governments, regulatory bodies and healthcare providers. Hopefully, once these studies exist, production processes can be streamlined and regulatory predictability can be enhanced. This could then lead to the implementation of policies that promote the sustainable supply of hormone treatments and open up environmentally friendly, more local, production and innovation that can serve the needs of half of the ageing population.

Geographers are also well equipped to study the scalar process of the politics of menopausing. Multiscalar inquiries could unpack how members of menopause and gynaecological societies, as well as politicians, lawmakers and decision makers, achieve legitimacy of decisions which impact lives of more than the half the world's population now or will have impacts in the future. Through inquiries into material products, geographers too can make interventions on what kinds of product (both hormone and non-hormone treatments, but ubiquitously used, such as melatonin to address sleep difficulties) are licenced and used in certain countries and how they are geographically distributed, regionally and locally. Equally, research that follows the flows of 'menopause' goods is critically needed. For instance, with freedom of movement within the EU, and including freedom of travel to and from Spain, the Nordic countries and others, midlife personal stories and books are full of episodes of how people engage in travel to use menopause services or buy goods elsewhere. With internet ordering, large amounts of supplements travel across borders, and numerous nutritionist and lifestyle blogs, books and podcasts point towards active use of diverse non-hormone supplements in midlife.

Conclusion

Feminist health geographies, and their research strands on the pill – hormonal contraception – birthing and menstruation have demonstrated a paradigm shift in women's lives, population demography, scalar process and geographic distinctiveness of reproduction (Connell and Walton-Roberts 2016; England et al 2019). Furthering the social strand on health geographies, but even more importantly the concepts that deal with power and emancipation, geographers can significantly advance the study of menopausing. Mahler and Pessar's (2001) gendered geographies of power can serve as a model for critical feminist geographies and illuminate how existing silences have kept menopausing people out of sight (ushered into invisible and quiet spaces in disciplinary siloes). Intersectional geographies can illuminate research voids on menopause in the geography of ageing and social difference scholarship in order to integrate the multiplicity of menopausing as a sociospatial process and legitimizing process of menopause recognition and treatment across the scales.

Moreover, geographers are equipped with theoretical and practical tools to unpack the flows and supply chains of menopause-related goods. Ultimately, the questions of menopause activism that advance menopause awareness and social change across countries, social differences and spaces, including through understanding of the human–non-human and intra-body scale relationship (what oestrogen does to a body and the environment), are waiting to be explored beyond strictly medical and biological frames. Some are actively seeking alternative spaces and networks that nurture resistance to the medically oppressive concept of menopause (Gambaudo 2017; Moore 2022). These topics will help to advance empirical research on menopausing experiences in diverse geographical contexts and on different scales, from lived experiences to the controversies of hormone and non-hormone approaches to the politics of menopausing and how legitimacy is constructed to achieve social change. These questions can guide innovative methodologies and further the application of feminist geography concepts in research on human and more-than-human relations, supply chains and activism studies. Ultimately, these approaches will advance the social scholarship of menopause through theories of gender, ageing and social change. Studying how middle-aged people want and can receive and give support and care in dignified terms suited to them is, therefore, a consequential feminist undertaking.

SIX

Conclusions: Policy Focus

Introduction

This chapter offers key conclusions and a policy focus in the hope of going some way to bridging the large gap between youth and older age studies and, thus, addressing the relative lack of geographical curiosity about midlife which has prevented us from seeing the diversity of middle-aged people and the plurality of their lifecourses over time and space. In this short book, it was not my aim to provide a thorough analysis; instead, I wanted to issue an invitation to: look with curiosity at midlife bodies, transitions, spaces and being in the middle of the lifecourse; and join the efforts to push forward this fascinating research field. I emphasize that midlife can neither be hollowed out by perpetuating demands for youthfulness nor 'swallowed' by the increasing tide of literature advancing older age geographies. The in-betweenness of this concept is a strength for geographical enquiry and policies that aim to improve people's capabilities.

Between youth and ageing geographies

'Knowledge is a social creation', claim Monk and Hanson (1982) in their famous article 'On not excluding half of the human in human geography'. It is not surprising, given their analysis of the history of gender research in geography, that we need to be critical towards omissions of midlife in knowledge production. Midlife geographies, similarly, have been largely overlooked in the discipline despite midlife being a highly complex and pivotal stage in the lifecourse that produces spaces and practices through intergenerational relations (Hopkins and Pain 2007). This is not because we do not have a specific definition of midlife. I do not think that it is useful to provide a strict, fixed definition of midlife which would clearly mark this lifecourse stage between youth and older age. In terms of what midlife is, the answer would be that it is a contingent construct. As such, it is important to understand how it was academically invented and what the consequences are of this invention. Intergenerational time, temporality and timing, seen through 'markers' of midlife events or transitions – all affect and shape the layers of the concept of midlife.

In terms of temporality, timing and chronological age, these temporal boundaries are at once fluid, arbitrary, deterministic (from statistical and policy points of view), normatively institutionalized and subjectively felt (Elder 1994; Lanchman 2001; Hörschelmann 2011; Infurna et al 2020; Hawkins and Haapio-Kirk 2023). Infurna et al (2020) state that the usual perception is that the chronological age of midlife is 40–60, flexibly adding or removing a decade or so either way. Midlife could be seen as the mid-point in the lifespan, as Baruch and Brooks-Gunn (1984) defined it four decades ago. However, the precise age is of little importance, as is true of the concepts of youth and old age. The very debate and awkwardness of trying to fix a chronological age reveals broader temporal contingencies and temporal boundaries, which are also of interest to geographers. People engage in 'boundary work' when trying to place themselves and others into certain normative categories related to body, work, care duties and social location. Policies, too, engage in such boundary work, although this largely applies to youth policies and support, which tend to be restricted to certain upper limits of age, which in turn begin at some imagined age boundary.

Another classic way to layer the concept of midlife is to use the term 'markers' in psychological and demographic studies of midlife (Baruch and Brooks-Gunn 1984: 14). However, such markers are very diverse and change over time. For instance, getting a stable job and establishing one's own home is a marker of the end of youth and the transition to the beginning of adulthood (Arnett 2001). Another marker, frequently used for midlife, is the 'empty nest' trope, meaning the changes to home practices associated with children leaving the home. However, researchers have long admitted – since the 1980s in fact – that it may not be useful to deterministically state specific markers of midlife, except from the marked gendered experience of the onset of menopause.

Of more importance are events. These can be called transitions, or they can be better approached as dynamic processes. There is a long-standing discussion on whether midlife has specific transitions. Staudinger and Bluck (2001), in their explanation relating midlife to processes of socialization, lay out why midlife tends to be overlooked in academic studies. As these authors note, from the policy point of view, midlife is seen as unproblematic. Policy makers usually emphasize the need for youth to be integrated and supported in order that they get education and then a job, then move into more stable careers and have access to the housing market. Hence, youth is seen as 'becoming adult' (Worth 2009). Adults, like those in midlife, from this policy perspective, do not need to be supported in their socialization. However, transitions, perhaps, are not that useful a concept for midlife, because this period of life is so rich with complex events, affecting people differently, along with social and geographic difference. Rather, as Infurna et al (2020) suggest, research could focus on specific events, such as unemployment, illness, divorce, disability, volatile labour markets and care duties for children or the older generation, and then discern how these events affect life satisfaction and what policy interventions could be made to tackle the potential negative effects on certain groups of middle-aged people in the places they live during these specific macro-level temporalities.

The political and economic events that shape intergenerational time are important for lifecourses (Giddens 1984). To illustrate the point, Baruch and Brooks-Gunn (1984) examined the Radcliffe study in the US, which involved women who graduated from Radcliffe College in 1947 and 1962. The research took place at the time of students' 20- and 30-year college reunions. The macro time events had significantly shaped the lifecourses of these two cohorts. The group that graduated in 1947 had grown up through the economic depression and studied during the Second World War. These respondents were surprised at how unprepared they were for midlife. The economic and political events they lived through contributed greatly to uncertainty. In comparison, those who graduated in 1962 were better prepared, had established careers and planned for the future. These findings matter for the research I have presented in the pages of this book. Most of the Latvian people in my research were born in the 1960s and 1970s. Their generational consciousness, drawing on Mannheim (1952), was shaped by spending their childhoods in the stagnation and later years of socialism, with planning policies that allocated jobs for everyone, severely restricted mobility and ideologically claimed that communism would be reached within the next few rounds of five-year plans. That never happened. Instead, that generation's identity and youth experiences were further shaped by the turbulence of post-socialism and its redistribution of property, rising unemployment, rapidly increasing social and geographical inequality, unforeseen career and professional opportunities under capitalism and, as I have demonstrated, migration as a strategy to achieve a better life. The political and economic contexts in certain places therefore give an insight into how important macro temporal factors are in shaping lifecourses.

Transitions and processes: body, work, home and relationships

Taking the theoretical discussions into account, I turned to what I have researched for more than a decade: the value of lived experience. I prioritized the ways of looking at midlife from the point of view of people themselves. I was trying to capture daily routines, taken-for-granted moments and the tactics people adopt in their use of space (de Certeau 1984) which allow them to contemplate the value of stability and security in everyday life (Stenning et al 2021). Lived experience is valuable because it shifts our understandings of the world and our place in it. Lived experience provides insights into how complex, plural and challenging lifecourses are and how the assumptions about stable lifecourses and linear upward mobility and earnings influence those whose real-life directions are far more diverse. The scales of body and home and the processes of work and linked lives are sharply gendered. They are influenced by macro events and shaped, to a greater extent, by ideas of what a good life could mean in midlife.

In contrast to examining indicators in large-scale datasets, with pre-defined questions and responses for what midlife is and how people are 'managing' their lives, I observed and engaged in multiple conversations, interviewing people using an unstructured interview format. Along with the aspects theoretically assumed to be distinctive to midlife – care, generativity and relationships (Lanchman 2001) – four cornerstones of midlife experience crystallized through the lenses of temporality and spatiality. These are bodies, work, home and linked lives.

I propose that the body, a long-standing scale of interest for feminist geographers and beyond, can be studied both as a midlife transition and as complex processes that reconfigure relationships with other people and places. The discourses of our era range from biopolitical and neoliberal calls to 'fix' bodies so that they fit into cultures of high achievement, are resilient to stress, look good, eat well and prepare good meals for the family. Widespread neuroculture, in particular, calls for us to optimize our brains and produce space via biopower (cf Foucault 1998), instead of creating conditions for plural epistemologies of midlife experience. Extant lifecourse theories overlook body needs. This omission has led to a lack of understanding of what body needs are and how diverse body experiences can be when producing relational spaces in midlife. In the meantime, the current lack of attention to body needs has created a space where health supplements, which make a wide range of promises that cannot be fulfilled, bring in billions due to ageism bias. Ideologies such as 'active ageing' (Walker 2002) could learn a lot from insights into lived bodily experiences in midlife in order to fine-tune the currently rather neoliberal focus on more caring, long-term and socially supported ageing that begins with midlife body transitions.

I also propose that attention to work during midlife shows that there is far more diversity of experience than just the assumed career peaks and maximal income (see MIDUS nd). The lived experience reveals a more complex landscape than that suggested by the White, middle-class sedentary focus, which has been treated as a reference for what good living looks like in midlife. My insights are admittedly limited due to the qualitative nature of work I do, and they are also different from classic approaches to midlife because I study migrants. However, these limitations and different approaches do not prevent me from seeing how complex midlife work processes are. People can peak in their careers if there are structural systems in place to support career growth. However, many people live below the limits of their capabilities, laying low and feeling stuck in midlife in order to maintain stable income and workplace because they feel that change could be too risky. A deliberate change of job in midlife is rather a privilege and indeed involves many risks to stability in older age.

I propose too that along with well-known and geographically advanced research agendas on linked lives, we need to pay attention to mundane but sometimes also dramatic home processes during midlife. Much of generativity (caring for and developing the capabilities of the younger generation) revolves around the home. Home in midlife is also a focal point for class ramifications. In the case of Latvian research participants, most desires and anxieties in midlife revolve about home, which is confirmed with, albeit still scant but alarming, warnings in other research that home insecurity has profound effects on relationships and on both physical and mental health in midlife (Robinson and Moen 2000; Sharam 2017; Bhat et al 2022).

Understanding working lives in midlife

In terms of policy focus, people's work life is the key aspect of midlife. In considering this aspect, it is important to understand that midlife is a pivotal life stage with strong relations to younger and older generations. The responsibility and ability to care for family and contribute to society are at their highest in the mid-lifecourse, as are the pressures to fulfil multiple roles. Work policies are the most important in creating structural support for those who are caring for others.

There is increasing pressure from businesses and public organizations to reskill and upskill. For instance, the World Economic Forum (2020) forecast that by 2050, up to 50 per cent of current professions and skill types could be redundant, obsolete or require significant reskilling. Even if forecasts are promising (as well as ominous), we should not ignore those middle-aged people who increasingly live in contexts of social insecurity and population ageing. Combined with their job insecurity and distress, often alongside childcare needs (as people in Western countries tend to have children later in life, in their thirties and early forties), middle-aged people do not welcome such a top-down prognosis. While such research and policies are often driven by market needs, people-centred approaches that focus on individuals' capabilities and learning in specific configurations of time and space are essential for informing democratic policies.

Infurna et al (2020) emphasize that financial vulnerabilities are increasing among middle-aged Americans, and disproportionally affect ethnic minority groups, gender-diverse people and those with low socioeconomic status. Financial insecurity leads to home insecurity and foreshadows a poorer and more precarious old age. Labour market volatility and economic recession further affect people's abilities to save for retirement and secure income for the needs of their children, and this is true even without mentioning underemployment and unemployment in midlife. Further, in many countries, being in work is a prerequisite to having medical insurance, which is something that becomes more important with the onset of midlife. Uninsured and underinsured midlife is a highly precarious situation, and when combined with reduced social and medical access, it is alarming. Also relevant here is inadequate policy intervention for unpaid and unsupported care, which many midlifers provide for their ageing and frail relatives.

There is a growing trend to move people's minds towards entrepreneurship as a response to market volatilities and individual needs for more flexible work schedules and, honestly, because of the ageism bias that is widespread in the labour market. Programmes for middle-aged entrepreneurs, aged 50 and above, exist in some countries in an attempt to support the entrepreneurial intentions of midlifers (Kautonen et al 2011). The push to entrepreneurship among migrants is particularly pronounced because of the combined bias of ageism and migrant status. In addition, migrants themselves support each other with business ideas when their immigration and visa statuses change in midlife, although they still have almost two decades of work ahead of them (Amrith 2022). However, we need to remain critical, instead of celebrating such a market push into individual entrepreneurship in midlife, not least due to ageism. According to Kibler et al (2015), starting a business in middle age can work out only in the relational process of individuals' capabilities and their willingness to adopt this approach, and only if existing social structures and governance support businesses and provide medical insurance and social safety nets for entrepreneurs.

More promising and far more challenging policies that could make a difference in the midlife world of work are those related to the ideas and methodologies of the four-day week (Kamerāde et al 2019; 2020). Research on this topic has shown that people and companies that participated in four-day week programmes did the same amount of work as they usually did in five days. Both employers and employees gained from the programme. Stenning et al (2021) provide feminist arguments for reducing the typical work week to four days which suggest that such changes can greatly improve daily lives and remedy the chronic care deficit in capitalist societies. Furthermore, this perspective, along with labour and feminist geographers' arguments, are far more wide-reaching than the idea of individual recuperation from paid labour in order to care more. This approach does not advocate working harder in four days so the worker can rest and regain the strength to work the next week. The four-day week is about organizing work differently and receiving the same salary. The experiments, across several countries, demonstrate that such arrangements reduce stress and, in turn, increase work and life satisfaction among employees, for instance, in Iceland (Kamerāde et al 2020).

Menopausing and gender equality

I have demonstrated in this book that menopausing (the period when hormonal changes start to affect ways of life) is a significant process that reorders relationships, spaces and temporalities. There has been a long history, indeed too long, of putting women in their place (Domosh and Seager 2001) and not addressing the reality of menopause, but now attention to this midlife body transition is gaining momentum. As DeLyser and Shaw (2013: 505) wisely said, menopause geographies need to be 'exhumated' from histories and disciplinary siloes. It is not the case that attention to menopausing has appeared on the agenda only recently. Historical research on feminist archives could, undoubtedly, unearth treasures of diverse and more caring ways to approach it than silencing practices might suggest. However, historically, market- and profit-oriented practices of hormone treatment have been more visible. The generation who were in their fifties and sixties before the new millennium remember the widely proposed hormone treatments that were taken up by many. The next generation, after the publication of the Women's Health Initiative data in 2002 suggesting that hormone treatment causes severe illnesses and early death, radically reduced use of hormone treatment (Brown 2012).

Menopause workplace frameworks already exist in some places and countries. They are becoming increasingly common in the UK but they are not yet widespread in Finland or Latvia. The building blocks for policies are based on gender difference and dynamic needs throughout the lifecourse. While pregnancy and parental leave policies are common and making some adjustments around childbirth is taken for granted, gender and lifecourse policies and initiatives are neither straightforward nor geographically even. For instance, policies on breastfeeding are rather scarce, and breastfeeding in public is still a marker of the gender struggle and of an achievement that is not yet widespread in Western countries (Williams et al 2021). Some organizations also have policies related to menstrual leave. Baird et al (2021), for example, have mapped legislation and policy history globally, showing how gender equality can be increased through entitlement and reinforcement for menstrual leave when it is necessary. Yet, the practical achievements in everyday workspaces are still highly limited. The same applies to openness and discourses around menstruation, which is a fundamental and ubiquitous experience for half the population. It is still far easier to say that you suffer headaches and therefore need rest and flexible work arrangements than it is to be open about pain, cramps and nausea due to menstruation (Clansy 2022).

Menopause policies, arguably, can be even more challenging due to long-standing taboo and silencing in the workplace (Grandey et al 2020). Developing crucial aspects of the built environment, such as ensuring appropriate access to toilets, maintaining a suitable temperature in the workspace, providing ventilation and creating places to rest, is important for the different types of work that menopausing people do. Most workplaces and work schedules are simply masculine-structured and not required to take into account gender and lifecourse diversity. This applies across all types of job and physical workplace, from public sector jobs to executive roles and from manual jobs to medical doctor roles. In the Canadian context, O'Hearn (2022) has demonstrated how physiotherapists, who, among others, help and treat menopausal people with diverse signs and symptoms of ill-being, themselves are in workplaces and work conditions that put strain on bodies and have significant consequences for their wellbeing.

The UK is at the forefront of many countries in the campaign for change. Some private organizations and businesses, along with public offices and universities, are making commitments to improve workplaces. Indeed, even some visible change in the built environment of the workplace, such as adding more toilets or a shower at work, can make a difference. Similarly, having code of ethics at work or an equality, diversity and inclusion (EDI) policy or non-discrimination policy that states people who are menopausing will be treated respectfully and their needs will be accommodated is important. These documents can make change happen in workplaces and help change spread across the country. As an example of this change, the British government has embarked on discussion and action plans relating to menopause policies (Adu 2023).

However, the challenges should not be underestimated. Just talking about menopause raises awareness, but investment in making space and time is a different matter. While firms can be motivated to fulfil EDI requirements and even innovate with diversity and inclusion through recognition of menopause, gender equality changes need to be wider-reaching. For instance, British activists (Menopause Mandate nd) together with medical doctors achieved an unprecedented step in 2023 when the National Health Service started providing certificates for hormone treatment that will make it affordable for most who need it. The same activists also demonstrate how geographically unequal access to treatment is in the UK, resembling the lines of the deeply entrenched North–South divide. This is one of the world's developed, centre economy countries, and it has highly developed antiracism and antidiscrimination policies covering protected characteristics. Campaigning for inclusion of menopause as one of these characteristics requires far more work to 'exhume' (cf DeLyser and Shaw 2013: 505) menopause knowledge, cultures, struggles and silences, because considering this highly pivotal midlife process without diverse insights into lived lives could lead to menopause becoming a buzzword, an empty shell or, worse, an unintended tool to 'other' menopausing people through deep-seated structures and practices of ageism, sexism and patriarchy.

Yet, a combination of bodily stress and psychosocial factors, along with care needs, do lead to job loss and burnout, which mean higher economic losses, even by strictly capitalist calculations of losses and gains. One way forward, I propose, would be to use the power of feminist geographies, especially those dealing with activism, to advance menopausing research agendas. It is imperative to theorize both positive and negative outcomes that reproduce patriarchy, commercialization and superficial gains for equality and diversity policies or working from home, as many continue to do after the COVID-19 pandemic. With a billion menopausing people globally, this is a public health and wellbeing issue that awaits the concerted efforts of research and activism.

References

Aboim, S. and Vasconcelos, P. (2020) Reassessing (de) standardisation: Life course trajectories across three generations, *Portuguese Journal of Social Science*, 18(3): 299–318.

Adu, A. (2023) Labour says it will urge UK firms to publish menopause action plan, *The Guardian*, 28 February, www.theguardian.com/society/2023/feb/28/labour-pledge-paid-time-off-and-workplace-support-for-menopause

Ahmed, A. and Hall, K. (2016) Negotiating the challenges of aging as a British migrant in Spain, *The Journal of Gerontopsychology and Geriatric Psychiatry*, 29(2): 105–114.

Albertson, E. (2021) *Rock Your Midlife: 7 Steps to Transform Yourself and Make Your Next Chapter Your Best Chapter*, North Hero, VT: Tiger Wellness Books, Kindle edition.

Alspaugh, A., Im, E., Reibel, D.M. and Barroso, J. (2021) The reproductive health priorities, concerns, and needs of women in midlife: A feminist poststructuralist qualitative analysis, *Qualitative Health Research*, 31(4): 643–653.

Amini, E. (2023) *Menopause in Iranian Muslim Women*, Cham: Palgrave Macmillan.

Amini, E. and McCormack, M. (2019) Medicalization, menopausal time and narratives of loss: Iranian Muslim women negotiating gender, sexuality and menopause in Tehran and Karaj, *Women's Studies International Forum*, 76: 102277. doi: 10.1016/j.wsif.2019.102277

Amnesty International (2023) *'I Know I Won't Get Help': Inequality of Healthcare in Finland*, London: Amnesty International, www.amnesty.org/en/documents/eur20/6899/2023/en/#:~:text=Based%20on%20extensive%20background%20research,left%20the%20Finnish%20healthcare%20system

Amrith, M. (2022) The temporal borders of transnational belonging: Aging migrant domestic workers in Singapore, *American Behavioral Scientist*, 66(14): 1912–1927.

Anderson, B. (2011) Affect and biopower: Towards a politics of life, *Transactions of the Institute of British Geographers*, 37(1): 28–43.

Appadurai, A. (2013) *The Future as Cultural Fact: Essays on the Global Condition*, New York: Verso.

Aririguzo, C., Spencer, B.S. and Freysteinson, W. (2022) 'You're acting womanish!' A qualitative descriptive study of the experiences of African American women in menopausal transition, *Journal of Women and Aging*, 34(2): 258–275.

Arnett, J.J. (2001) Conceptions of the transition to adulthood: Perspectives from adolescence through midlife, *Journal of Adult Development*, 8(2): 133–143.

Arpanantikul, M. (2006) Self-care process as experienced by middle-aged Thai women, *Health Care for Women International*, 27(10): 893–907.

Atkinson, C., Ford, J., Harding, N. and Jones, F. (2015) The expectations and aspirations of a late-career professional woman, *Work, Employment and Society*, 29(6): 1019–1028.

Atkinson, C., Beck, V., Brewis, J., Davies, A. and Duberley, J. (2021) Menopause and the workplace: New directions in HRM research and HR practice, *Human Resource Management Journal*, 31(1): 49–64.

Atkinson, C., Carmichael, F. and Duberley, J. (2021) The menopause taboo at work: Examining women's embodied experiences of menopause in the UK police service, *Work, Employment and Society*, 35(4): 657–676.

Avis, N.E., Stellato, R., Crawford, S., Bromberger, J., Ganz, P., Cain, V. and Kagawa-Singer, M. (2001) Is there a menopausal syndrome? Menopausal status and symptoms across racial/ethnic groups, *Social Science & Medicine*, 52(3): 345–356.

Bailey, A.J. (2009) Population geography: Lifecourse matters, *Progress in Human Geography*, 33(3): 407–418.

Baird, M., Hill, E. and Colussi, S. (2021) Mapping menstrual leave legislation and policy historically and globally: A labor entitlement to reinforce, remedy, or revolutionize gender equality at work? *Comparative Labour Law and Policy Journal*, 42(1): 187–225.

REFERENCES

Baker, E., Bentley, R. and Mason, K. (2013) The mental health effects of housing tenure: Causal or compositional? *Urban Studies*, 50(2): 426–442.

Baldassar, L. and Merla, L. (2014) *Transnational Families, Migration and the Circulation of Care: Understanding Mobility and Absence in Family Life*, London and New York: Routledge.

Barrett, A.E. (2005) Gendered experiences in midlife: Implications for age identity, *Journal of Aging Studies*, 19(2): 163–183.

Barry, E. (2019) Endogenous misery: menopause in medicine, literature and culture, in A. King, K. Almack and R.L. Jones (eds) *Intersections of Ageing, Gender and Sexualities: Multidisciplinary International Perspectives* (online edn), Bristol, Policy Press Scholarship Online. doi: 10.1332/policypress/9781447333029.003.0006

Barton, D. (2023) *Midlife Battle Cry: Redefining the Mighty Second Half*, Nashville, TN: Thomas Nelson.

Baruch, E. and Brooks-Gunn, J. (1984) *Women in Midlife*, New York and London: Plenum Press.

Bassel, L. (2012) *Refugee Women: Beyond Gender versus Culture*, London: Routledge.

Bastia, T. (2019) *Gender, Migration and Social Transformation: Intersectionality in Bolivian Itinerant Migrations*, London and New York: Routledge.

Bastia, T., Lulle, A. and King, R. (2022) Migration and development: The overlooked roles of older people and ageing, *Progress in Human Geography*, 46(4): 1009–1027.

Bate, B. (2018) Understanding the influence tenure has on meanings of home and homemaking practices, *Geography Compass*, 12(1): e12354. doi: 10.1111/gec3.12354

Bauman, Z. (2001) *The Individualized Society*, Cambridge: Polity Press.

Baxter, R. and Brickell, K. (2014) For home unmaking, *Home Cultures*, 11(2): 133–143.

Bellipanni, G.F.D.I.M., Di Marzo, F., Blasi, F. and Di Marzo, A. (2005) Effects of melatonin in perimenopausal and menopausal women: Our personal experience, *Annals of the New York Academy of Sciences*, 1057(1): 393–402.

Bhakta, A., Reed, B. and Fisher, J. (2019) Behind closed doors: The hidden needs of perimenopausal women in Ghana, in M. England, M. Fannin and H. Hazen (eds) *Reproductive Geographies* (pp 67–88), London: Routledge.

Bhat, A.C., Almeida, D.M., Fenelon, A. and Santos-Lozada, A.R. (2022) A longitudinal analysis of the relationship between housing insecurity and physical health among midlife and aging adults in the United States, *SSM-Population Health*, 18: 101128. doi: 10.1016/j.ssmph.2022.101128

Billings, J. (2018) *Midlife Crisis in Men: How to Overcome a Male Midlife Crisis and Rediscover the Real You in 12 Steps*, Kindle edition.

Binfa, L., Castelo-Branco, C., Blümel, J.E., Cancelo, M.J., Bonilla, H., Muñoz, I., … and Ríos, R.V. (2004) Influence of psychosocial factors on climacteric symptoms, *Maturitas*, 48(4): 425–431.

Blackie, S. (2022) *Hagitude: Reimagining the Second Half of Life*, Novato, CA: New World Library.

Blunt, A. (2005) Cultural geography: Cultural geographies of home, *Progress in Human Geography*, 29(4): 505–515.

Blunt, A. and Varley, A. (2004) Geographies of home, *Cultural Geographies*, 11(1): 3–6.

Blunt, A. and Dowling, R. (2006) *Home*, London: Routledge.

Boston Women's Health Collective (2006) *Our Bodies, Ourselves*, Chicago, IL: Boston Women's Health Collective.

Boyer, K., Eaves, L.E. and Fluri, J. (eds) (2023) *Activist Feminist Geographies*, Bristol: Policy Press.

Brickell, K. (2012) 'Mapping' and 'doing' critical geographies of home, *Progress in Human Geography*, 36(2): 225–244.

Brooks-Gunn, J. and Kirsh, B. (1984) Life events and the boundaries of midlife for women, in G. Baruch and J. Brooks-Gunn (eds) *Women in Midlife* (pp 11–30), Boston, MA: Springer.

Brown, S. (2012) Shock, terror and controversy: How the media reacted to the Women's Health Initiative, *Climacteric: The Journal of the International Menopause Society*, 15(3): 275–280.

Butler, C. (2020) Managing the menopause through 'abjection work': When boobs can become embarrassingly useful, again, *Work, Employment and Society*, 34(4): 696–712.

REFERENCES

Carr, D. (2018) The linked lives principle in life course studies: Classic approaches and contemporary advances, in D. Alwin, D. Felmlee and D. Kreager (eds) *Social Networks and the Life Course: Frontiers in Sociology and Social Research*, vol 2 (pp 41–65), Cham: Springer.

Carter, S., Davis, S. and Black, K.I. (2021) Menopause workplace policy: The way forward or backward? *Australian and New Zealand Journal of Obstetrics and Gynaecology*, 61(6): 986–989.

Clancy, K. (2022) *Period: The Real Story of Menstruation*, Princeton, NJ: Princeton University Press.

Clarke, J. and Kearns, A. (2012) Housing improvements, perceived housing quality and psychosocial benefits from the home, *Housing Studies*, 27(7): 915–939.

Connell, J. and Walton-Roberts, M. (2016) What about the workers? The missing geographies of health care, *Progress in Human Geography*, 40(2): 158–176. doi: 10.1177/0309132515570513

Cranston, S. (2017) Self-help and the surfacing of identity: Producing the third culture kid, *Emotion, Space and Society*, 24: 27–33.

Crenshaw, K. (1991) Mapping the margins: Intersectionality, identity politics, and violence against women of color, *Stanford Law Review*, 43(6): 1241–1299.

Davidson, J., Bondi, L. and Smith, M. (2016) *Emotional Geographies*, London: Routledge.

Davis, R.H. (1981) The middle years, in R.H. Davis (ed) *Aging: Prospects and Issues* (3rd edn, pp 201–233), Los Angeles: Andrus Gerontology Center.

De Beauvoir, S. (1949/2011) *The Second Sex*, translated by C. Borde and S. Malovany-Chevallier, New York: Vintage.

de Certeau, M. (1984) *The Practice of Everyday Life*, Berkeley, CA: University of California Press.

Delanoë, D., Hajri, S., Bachelot, A., Mahfoudh, D., Hassoun, D., Marsicano, E. and Ringa, V. (2012) Class, gender and culture in the experience of menopause: A comparative survey in Tunisia and France, *Social Science & Medicine*, 75(2): 401–409.

Del Casino, V.J., Jr (2009) *Social Geography*, Chichester: Wiley-Blackwell.

DeLyser, D. and Shaw, W. (2013) For menopause geographies, *Area*, 45(4): 504–506.

De Mello, A., Chavez, A., Mukarram, M., Buras, M.R. and Kling, J.M. (2021). Menopausal symptoms in the Southwest United States: A cross-sectional survey of women from areas with different socioeconomic resources, *Maturitas*, 154: 7–12.

Department of Health and Social Care (2023) The government's 2023 mandate to NHS England, *GOV.UK*, www.gov.uk/government/publications/nhs-mandate-2023/the-governments-2023-mandate-to-nhs-england

Dibonaventura, M.F., Chandran, A., Hsu, M.-A. and Bushmakin, A. (2013) Burden of vasomotor symptoms in France, Germany, Italy, Spain, and the United Kingdom, *International Journal of Women's Health*, 5: 261–269.

Doel, M. and Sergott, J. (2003) Self, health, and gender: Complementary and alternative medicine in the British mass media, *Gender, Place & Culture*, 10(2): 131–144.

Domosh, M. and Seager, J. (2001) *Putting Women in Place: Feminist Geographers Make Sense of the World*, New York: Guilford Press.

Dratva, J., Gómez Real, F., Schindler, C., Ackermann-Liebrich, U., Gerbase, M.W., Probst-Hensch, N.M., … and Zemp, E. (2009) Is age at menopause increasing across Europe? Results on age at menopause and determinants from two population-based studies, *Menopause*, 16(2): 385–394.

Du Bois-Reymond, M. and López Blasco, A. (2003) Yo-yo transitions and misleading trajectories: Towards integrated transition policies for young adults in Europe, in A. López Blasco, W. McNeish and A. Walther (eds) *Young People and Contradictions of Inclusion: Towards Integrated Transition Policies in Europe* (pp 19–41), Bristol: Policy Press.

Duncan, M. (2004) Autoethnography: Critical appreciation of an emerging art, *International Journal of Qualitative Methods*, 3(4): 28–39.

Durham, D. (2008) Apathy and agency: The romance of agency and youth in Botswana, in J. Cole and D. Durham (eds) *Figuring the Future: Globalisation and the Temporalities of Children and Youth* (pp 151–178), Santa Fe, NM: SAR Press.

REFERENCES

Edwards, A.L., Shaw, P.A., Halton, C.C., Bailey, S.C., Wolf, M.S., Andrews, E.N. and Cartwright, T. (2021) 'It just makes me feel a little less alone': A qualitative exploration of the podcast Menopause: Unmuted on women's perceptions of menopause, *Menopause*, 28(12): 1374–1384.

Eisler, R. (1988) *The Chalice and the Blade: Our History, Our Future*, New York: HarperCollins.

Elder, G.H. (1994) Time, human agency, and social change: Perspectives on the life course, *Social Psychology Quarterly*, 57(1): 4–15.

Elder, G.H., Johnson, M.K. and Crosnol, R. (2003) The emergence and development of life course theory, in J.T. Mortimer and M.J. Shanahan (eds) *Handbook of the Life Course* (pp 3–19), Cham: Springer.

Elkin, L. (2015) Private theory, *TLS*, 5878: 25–26.

England, M., Fannin, M. and Hazen, H. (eds) (2019) *Reproductive Geographies*, London: Routledge.

Erikson, E. (1980) *Identity and the Life Cycle*, New York: Norton.

Eurostat (2015) Being Young in Europe Today, European Union, https://ec.europa.eu/eurostat/documents/3217494/6776245/KS-05-14-031-EN-N.pdf

Eurostat (2020) Being young in Europe today – executive summary, https://ec.europa.eu/eurostat/statistics-explained/index.php?title=Being_young_in_Europe_today_-_executive_summary

Farrant, M. (2022) Autofiction, autotheory, and the neoliberal contemporary, *American Book Review*, 43(2): 63–67.

Ferrand, F., Hajri, S., Benzineb, S., Draoui, D.M., Hassoun, D., Delanoë, D. … and Ringa, V. (2013) Comparative study of the quality of life associated with menopause in Tunisia and France, *Menopause*, 20(6): 609–622.

Findlay, A., McCollum, D., Coulter, R. and Gayle, V. (2015) New mobilities across the life course: A framework for analysing demographically linked drivers of migration, *Population, Space Place*, 21(4): 390–402.

Flint, M. (1976) Cross-cultural factors that affect age of menopause, in P.A. van Keep, R.B. Greenblatt and M. Albeaux-Fernet (eds) *Consensus on Menopause Research* (pp 73–83), Dordrecht: Springer.

Flint, M.P. (1997) Secular trends in menopause age, *Journal of Psychosomatic Obstetrics & Gynaecology*, 18(2): 65–72.

Formenti, L. and West, L. (2018) *Transforming Perspectives of Lifelong Learning and Adult Education*, Cham: Palgrave Macmillan and Springer Nature.

Forstrup, M. and Smellie, A. (2021) *Cracking the Menopause: While Keeping Yourself Together*, London: Bluebird, Kindle edition.

Foucault, M. (1991) Governmentality, in G. Burchell, C. Gordon and P. Miller (eds) *The Foucault Effect: Studies in Governmentality, with Two Lectures by and an Interview with Michel Foucault* (pp 87–104), Chicago: University of Chicago Press.

Foucault, M. (1998) *The History of Sexuality Vol 1: The Will to Knowledge*, London: Penguin.

Frank, A.W. (1995/2013) *The Wounded Storyteller: Body, Illness and Ethics*, Chicago, IL: University of Chicago Press.

Gambaudo, S. (2017) The regulation of gender in menopause theory, *Topoi*, 36: 549–559.

Gecas, V. (2003) Self-agency and the life course, in J.T. Mortimer and M.J. Shanahan (eds) *The Handbook of Life Course* (pp 369–388), Cham: Springer.

Geertz, C. (1973) *The Interpretation of Cultures*, New York: Basic Books.

Gesler, W.M. and Kearns, R.A. (2002) *Culture/Place/Health*, London: Routledge.

Geukes, M., van Aalst, M.P., Nauta, M.C. and Oosterhof, H. (2012) The impact of menopausal symptoms on work ability, *Menopause*, 19(3): 278–282.

Giddens, A. (1984) *Constitution of Society*, Cambridge: Polity.

Giddens, A. (1991) *Modernity and Self-Identity: Self and Society in the Late Modern Age*, Stanford, CA: Stanford University Press.

Glyde, T. (2021) How can therapists and other healthcare practitioners best support and validate their queer menopausal clients? *Sexual Relationship Therapy*, 38(4): 510–532.

Glyde, T. (2022) LGBTQIA+ menopause: Room for improvement, *The Lancet*, 400(10363): 1578–1579.

Goodson, I., Loveless A. and Stephens D. (2012) *Explorations in Narrative Research*, Rotterdam: Sense Publishers.

REFERENCES

Grandey, A.A., Gabriel, A.S. and King, E.B. (2020) Tackling taboo topics: A review of the three Ms in working women's lives, *Journal of Management*, 46(1): 7–35.

Grenier, A., Phillipson, C. and Settersten, R. (eds) (2020) *Precarity and Ageing: Understanding Changing Forms of Risk and Vulnerability in Later Life*, Bristol: Policy Press.

Gullette, M.M. (2016) *Safe at Last in the Middle Years: The Invention of the Midlife Progress Novel*, Open Road Distribution, Kindle edition.

Gunter, J. (2021) *The Menopause Manifesto: Own Your Health with Facts and Feminism*, New York: Citadel Press.

Gupta, A. and Ferguson, J. (1997) *Anthropological Locations: Boundaries and Grounds of a Field Science*, Berkeley: University of California Press.

Haasler, S.R. and Hokema, A. (2022) Female solo self-employment in Germany: The role of transitions and learning from a life course perspective, *Social Inclusion*, 10(4): 150–160.

Hacking, M. and Mander, T. (2022) Menopause care: Political visions and UK Menopause Taskforce; heralding change? *Post Reproductive Health*, 28(2): 63–65.

Hammam, R.A., Abbas, R.A. and Hunter, M.S. (2012) Menopause and work: The experience of middle-aged female teaching staff in an Egyptian governmental faculty of medicine, *Maturitas*, 71(3): 294–300.

Harding, S. (1991) *Whose Science? Whose Knowledge?: Thinking from Women's Lives*, Ithaca, NY: Cornell University Press.

Hashiguchi, K., Yoshikawa, S. and Muto, T. (2021) Emotion regulation processes and middle-aged Japanese women's health, *Climacteric*, 24(2): 200–205.

Hawkins, C. and Haapio-Kirk, L. (2023) Bringing ageing to life: A comparative study of age categories, *Anthropology and Aging*, 44(2): 11–27.

Heinonen, P. (2021) *Hyvinvointia Vaihdevuosiin*, Helsinki: WSOY.

Higgs, P. and Gilleard, C. (2017) Ageing, dementia and the social mind: Past, present and future perspectives, *Sociology of Health and Illness*, 39(2): 175–181.

Hollis, J. (1993) *The Middle Passage: From Misery to Meaning in Mid-Life*, New York: Inner City Books.

Holloway, S.L., Holt, L. and Mills, S. (2019) Questions of agency: Capacity, subjectivity, spatiality and temporality, *Progress in Human Geography*, 43(3): 458–477.

hooks, b. (1988/2015) *Talking Back: Thinking Feminist, Thinking Black*, New York: Routledge.

Hopkins, P. and Pain, R. (2007) Geographies of age: Thinking relationally, *Area*, 39(3): 287–294.

Hörschelmann, K. (2011) Theorising life transitions: Geographical perspectives, *Area*, 43(4): 378–383.

Hulce, S. (2020) *A Well Done Professional Midlife Crisis: How to Bleed Passion & Energy Back Into Your Career*, Charleston, SC: Forbes, Kindle edition.

Infurna, F.J., Gerstorf, D. and Lachman, M.E. (2020) Midlife in the 2020s: Opportunities and challenges, *American Psychologist*, 75(4): 470–485.

Jack, G., Riach, K. and Bariola, E. (2019) Temporality and gendered agency: Menopausal subjectivities in women's work, *Human Relations*, 72(1): 122–143.

Jack, G., Riach, K., Hickey, M., Griffiths, A., Hardy, C. and Hunter, M. (2021) Menopause in the workplace: Building evidence, changing workplaces, supporting women, *Maturitas*, 151: 63–64.

Jamieson, A. (2022) *Midlife: Humanity's Secret Weapon*, La Vergne: Notting Hill Editions, Kindle edition.

Jang, S.Y., Oksuzyan, A., Myrskylä, M., van Lenthe, F.J. and Loi, S. (2023) *Healthy Immigrants, Unhealthy Ageing? Analysis of Health Decline among Older Migrants and Natives across European Countries*, Max Planck Institute for Demographic Research WP-2023-024, www.demogr.mpg.de/papers/working/wp-2023-024.pdf

Jaques, E. (1965) Death and the midlife crisis, *The International Journal of Psychoanalysis*, 46(4): 502–514.

Jones, R.L. (2011) Imaging old age, in J. Katz, S. Peace and S. Spurr (eds) *Adult Lives: A Life Course Perspective* (pp 18–26), Bristol: Policy Press.

Kajan, M. (2023) *Iloa ja terveyttä. Naisen vaihdevuodet ja hormonit*, Helsinki: Basam Books.

REFERENCES

Kamerāde, D., Wang, S., Burchell, B., Balderson, S.U. and Coutts, A. (2019) A shorter working week for everyone: How much paid work is needed for mental health and well-being? *Social Science & Medicine*, 241: 112353. doi: 10.1016/j.socscimed.2019.06.006

Kamerāde, D., Balderson, U., Burchell, B., Wang, S. and Coutts, A. (2020) *Shorter Working Week and Workers' Well-Being and Mental Health*, Centre for Business Research, University of Cambridge, Working Paper 522, www.jbs.cam.ac.uk/wp-content/uploads/2023/05/cbrwp522.pdf

Katz, C. and Monk, J. (1993) *Full Circles: Geographies of Women Over the Lifecourse*, London: Routledge.

Kautonen, T., Tornikoski, E.T. and Kibler, E. (2011) Entrepreneurial intentions in the third age: The impact of perceived age norms, *Small Business Economics*, 37: 219–234.

Kibler, E., Wainwright, T., Kautonen, T. and Blackburn, R. (2015) Can social exclusion against 'older entrepreneurs' be managed? *Journal of Small Business Management*, 53: 193–208.

King, A., Almack, K. and Jones, R.L. (2019) Introduction: Intersections of ageing, gender and sexualities, in A. King, K. Almack and R.L. Jones (eds) *Intersections of Ageing, Gender and Sexualities: Multidisciplinary International Perspectives* (online edn), Bristol: Policy Press Scholarship Online. doi: 10.1332/policypress/9781447333029.003.0001

Knoll, N. and Schwarzer, R. (2002) Gender and age differences in social support: A study of East German migrants heart disease, in G. Weidner, K. Kopp and M. Kristenson (eds) *Environment, Stress and Gender* (pp 72–91), Amsterdam: IOS Press.

Krajewski, S. (2018) Advertising menopause: You have been framed, *Continuum*, 33(1): 137–148.

Kraus, C. (1997/2006) *I Love Dick*, Los Angeles: Semiotext Native Agents Series.

Krivade, A. (2022) Dārgo lasītāj! (Dear reader!), A letter from the translator of C. Kraus *I love Dick*, Munich: btb Verlag, sold together with the translated book.

Lachman M.E. (ed) (2001) *Handbook of Midlife Development*, New York: Wiley and Sons, Inc.

Lavigne, V.D. and Finley, G.E. (1990) Memory in middle-aged adults, *Educational Gerontology*, 16(5): 447–461.

Lawson, J. (2011) Chronotope, story, and historical geography: Mikhail Bakhtin and the space-time of narratives, *Antipode*, 43(2): 384–412.

Levitt, P., Lloyd, C., Mueller, A. and Viterna, J. (2015) *Global Social Protection: Setting the Agenda,* Robert Schuman Centre for Advanced Studies Research Paper No 78.

Ley, D. (1977) Social geography and taken-for-granted world, *Transactions of the Insitute of British Geographer*, 2(4): 498–512.

Lock, M. (1993) *Encounters with Aging: Mythologies of Menopause in Japan and North America,* Berkeley and Los Angeles: University of California Press.

Loe, M. (2011) *Aging Our Way: Independent Elders, Interdependent Lives*, New York: Oxford University Press.

Longhurst, R. (2001) *Bodies: Exploring Fluid Boundaries*, London: Routledge.

Lopata, H.Z. and Barnewolt, D. (1984) The middle years: Changes and variations in social role commitments, in E. Baruch and J. Brooks-Gunn (eds) *Women in Midlife* (pp 83–108), New York and London: Plenum Press.

Lorde, A. (1980) *The Cancer Journals*, San Francisco, CA: Aunt Lute Books.

Lorde, A. (1997) Age, race, class, and sex: Women redefining difference, in A. McClintock, A. Mufti and E. Shohat (eds) *Dangerous Liaisons: Gender, Nation, and Postcolonial Perspectives* (pp 374–380), Minneapolis: University of Minnesota Press.

Lulle, A. (2014a) Shifting notions of gendered care and neoliberal motherhood: From lives of Latvian migrant women in Guernsey, *Women's Studies International Forum*, 47: 239–249.

Lulle, A. (2014b) Spaces of encounter-displacement: Contemporary labour migrants' return visits to Latvia, *Geografiska Annaler, B Series*, 96(2): 127–140.

Lulle, A. (2018) Relational ageing: on intra-gender and generational dynamism amongst ageing Latvian women, *Area*, 50(4): 452–458.

REFERENCES

Lulle, A. (2019) Ageing (im)mobilities: The lives of Latvian women who emigrated and those who stayed put, *Gender, Place and Culture*, 25(8): 1193–1208.

Lulle A. (2021) Reversing retirement frontiers in the spaces of post-socialism: Active ageing through migration for work, *Ageing and Society*, 41(6): 1308–1327.

Lulle, A. (2023) The affective fields of working-class among 'Eastern European' migrants in the UK, *The Sociological Review*, 71(2): 315–331.

Lulle, A., Moroşanu, L. and King, R. (2022) *Young EU Migrants in London in the Transition to Brexit*, London and New York: Routledge.

MacKenzie, R. and Marks, A. (2019) Older workers and occupational identity in the telecommunications industry: Navigating employment transitions through the life course, *Work, Employment and Society*, 33(1): 39–55.

Mahler, E.B. (2011) Midlife work role transitions: Generativity and learning in 21st-century careers, in C. Hoare (ed) *The Oxford Handbook of Reciprocal Adult Development and Learning* (pp 186–214), Oxford: Oxford University Press.

Mahler, S.J. and Pessar, P.R. (2001) Gendered geographies of power: Analyzing gender across transnational spaces, *Identities*, 7(4): 441–459.

Makuwa, G.N., Rikhotso, S.R. and Mulaudzi, F.M. (2015) The perceptions of African women regarding natural menopause in Mamelodi, Tshwane district, *Curationis*: 38(2), 1–7.

Mannheim, K. (1952) The problem of generations, in P.I. Kecskemeti (ed) *Karl Mannheim: Essays* (pp 276–320), London: Routledge.

Marso, L. (2019) Feminist cringe comedy: Dear Dick, the joke is on you, *Politics and Gender*, 15(1): 107–129.

Martins, R., de Sousa, B. and Rodrigues, V. (2022) The geography of the age at menopause in central Portugal since the early twentieth century, *Scientific Reports*, 12: 22020. doi: 10.1038/s41598-022-25475-w

Massey, D. (2005) *For Space*, London: Sage.

Matthews, J. (2016) *Midlife Manifesto: A Woman's Guide to Thriving after Forty*, New York: Skyhorse, Kindle edition.

May, J. and Thrift, N. (2001) *Timespace*, London: Routledge.

Mayer, K.U. (2004) Whose lives? How history, societies, and institutions define and shape life courses, *Research in Human Development*, 1(3): 161–187.

Mayer, K.U. (2009) New directions in life course research, *Annual Review of Sociology*, 35: 413–433.

McCall, D. and Potter, N. (2022) *Menopausing: The Positive Roadmap to Your Second Spring*, HarperCollins, Kindle edition.

McCarthy, M. and Raval, A.P. (2020) The peri-menopause in a woman's life: A systemic inflammatory phase that enables later neurodegenerative disease, *Journal of Neuroinflammation*, 17(1): 1–14.

Menopause Mandate (nd) www.menopausemandate.com

Midlarsky, E. and Nitzburg, G. (2008) Eating disorders in middle-aged women, *The Journal of General Psychology*, 135(4): 393–408.

MIDUS (nd) Midlife in the United States: A national longitudinal survey of health and well-being, University of Wisconsin-Madison, Institute of Aging, http://midus.wisc.edu/puboverview.php

Moen, P. (2003) Midcourse, in J.T. Mortimer and M.J. Shanahan (eds) *The Handbook of Life Course* (pp 269–291), Cham: Springer.

Monk, J. and Hanson, S. (1982) On not excluding half of the human in human geography, *The Professional Geographer*, 34(1): 11–23.

Montero, G.J., Ciancio de Montero, A.M. and Singman de Vogelfanger, L. (2019) *Updating Midlife: Psychoanalytic Perspectives*, London and New York: Routledge.

Moore, A. (2022) *The French Invention of Menopause and the Medicalisation of Women's Ageing*, Oxford: Oxford University Press.

Moroşanu, L., King, R., Lulle, A. and Pratsinakis, M. (2021) 'One improves here every day': The occupational and learning journeys of 'lower-skilled' European migrants in the London region, *Journal of Ethnic and Migration Studies*, 47(8): 1775–1792.

Morson, G.S. (2010) The chronotope of humanness: Bakhtin and Dostoevsky, in N. Bemong, P. Borghart, M. De Dobbeleer, K. Demoen, K. De Temmerman and B. Keunen (eds) *Bakhtin's Theory of the Literary Chronotope: Reflections, Applications, Perspectives* (pp 93–110), Gent: Academia Press. https://library.oapen.org/viewer/web/viewer.html?file=/bitstream/handle/20.500.12657/34655/377572.pdf?sequence=1&isAllowed=y

REFERENCES

N Muir, K. (2023) Menopause in the workplace with Kate Muir, NHS South West Youtube channel, 29 Mar. https://youtu.be/XZz6vM0AGQ4

Nappi, R.E., Siddiqui, E., Todorova, L., Rea, C., Gemmen, E. and Schultz, N.M. (2023) Prevalence and quality-of-life burden of vasomotor symptoms associated with menopause: A European cross-sectional survey, *Maturitas*, 167: 66–74.

National Institute for Health and Care Excellence (2023) Menopause: diagnosis and management, www.nice.org.uk/guidance/ng23

Nemiroff, R.A. and Colarusso, C.A. (eds) (1990) *New Dimensions in Adult Development*, New York: Basic Books/Hachette Book Group.

Newson, L. (2023) *The Definitive Guide to the Perimenopause and Menopause*, London: Yellow Kite, Kindle edition.

Ní Léime, Á., Street, D., Vickerstaff, S., Krekula, S. and Loretto, W. (eds) (2017) *Gender, Ageing and Extended Working Life: Cross-National Perspectives*, Bristol: Policy Press.

Ochs, S. (2015) *Midmen: The Modern Man's Guide to Surviving Midlife Crisis*, Kindle Edition.

Official Statistics Portal (Latvia) (2023) Long-term international migration, https://stat.gov.lv/en/statistics-themes/population/migration

O'Hearn, S. (2022) Place-Based Experiences in the Work Environment During the Menopausal Transition: A Case Study of Canadian Physiotherapists, PhD thesis, University of Waterloo, Ontario.

Palacios, S., Henderson, V.W., Siseles N., Tan, D. and Villaseca, P. (2010) Age of menopause and impact of climacteric symptoms by geographical region, *Climacteric*, 13(5): 419–428.

Panay, N., Palacios, S., Davison, S. and Baber, R. (2021) Women's perception of the menopause transition: A multinational, prospective, community-based survey, *Gynecological and Reproductive Endocrinology and Metabolism*, 2(3): 178–183.

Perrig-Chiello, P. and Perren, S. (2005) Biographical transitions from a midlife perspective, *Journal of Adult Development*, 12(4): 169–181.

Peterson, L.W. and Kiesinger, C.E. (2019) *Narrating Midlife: Crisis, Transition, and Transformation*, Lanham: Lexington Books.

Pile, S. (2010) Emotions and affect in recent human geography, *Transactions of the Institute of British Geographers*, 35(1): 5–20.

Pinkola Estés, C. (1992) *Women Who Run with the Wolves: Myths and Stories of the Wild Woman Archetype*, New York: Ballantine Books.

Pöllänen, P. and Davydova, O. (2017) Welfare, work and migration from a gender perspective: Back to 'family settings'? *Nordic Journal of Migration Research*, 7(4): 205–213.

Potter, J. (2020) The ghost of the stable path: Stories of work-life change at the 'end of career', *Work, Employment and Society*, 34(4): 571–586.

Prothero, L.S., Foster, T. and Winterson, D. (2021) 'Menopause affects us all ...': Menopause transition experiences of female ambulance staff from a UK ambulance service, *British Paramedic Journal*, 6(3): 41–48.

Queermenopause Collective (nd) Resources, queermenopause.com/resources

Re:Baltica (2022) *Karmas latvieši*, Investigative documentary, https://rebaltica.lv/

Rees, M., Lambrinoudaki, I., Cano, A. and Simoncini, T. (2019) Menopause: Women should not suffer in silence, *Maturitas*, 124: 91–92.

Riach, K. and Jack, G. (2021) Women's health in/and work: Menopause as an intersectional experience, *International Journal of Environmental Research and Public Health*, 18(20): 10793. doi: 10.3390/ijerph182010793

Robinson, J. and Moen, P. (2000) A life-course perspective on housing expectations and shifts in late midlife, *Research on Aging*, 22(5): 499–532.

Rose, G. (1993) *Feminism and Geography: The Limits of Geographical Knowledge*, Minneapolis: University of Minnesota Press.

Rose, G. (2007) *The Politics of Life: Biomedicine, Power and Subjectivity in the Twenty-First Century*, Princeton, NJ: Princeton University Press.

Rosenfeld, A. (2004) *Women's Health in Mid-Life. A Primary Care Guide*, Cambridge: University of Cambridge Press.

REFERENCES

Rubin, H.J. and Rubin, I.S. (2005) *Qualitative Interviewing: The Art of Hearing Data*, London: Sage.

Ryan, L. (2011) Migrants' social networks and weak ties: Accessing resources and constructing relationships post-migration, *The Sociological Review*, 59(4): 707–724.

Sandberg, L. (2013) Affirmative old age: The ageing body and feminist theories on difference, *International Journal of Ageing and Later Life*, 8(1): 11–40.

Saukko, P. (2000) Between voice and discourse: Quilting interviews on anorexia, *Qualitative Inquiry*, 6(3): 299–317.

Schatzki, T. and Natter, W. (1996) *The Social and Political Body*, New York: Guilford Press.

Scheinman, G. (2022) *The Midlife Male*, Amplify Publishing.

Schoenaker, D.A., Jackson, C.A., Rowlands, J.V. and Mishra, G.D. (2014) Socioeconomic position, lifestyle factors and age at natural menopause: A systematic review and meta-analyses of studies across six continents, *International Journal of Epidemiology*, 43(5): 1542–1562.

Schroot, T. (2022) Professional trajectories in migrant biographies of qualified German, Romanian, and Italian movers, *Social Inclusion*, 10(4): 138–149.

Setiya, K. (2010) *Midlife: A Philosophical Guide*, Princeton, NJ: Princeton University Press.

Sharam, A. (2017) The voices of midlife women facing housing insecurity in Victoria, Australia, *Social Policy and Society*, 16(1): 49–63. doi: 10.1017/S1474746415000603

Sharp, J. (2009) Geography and gender: What belongs to feminist geography? Emotion, power and change, *Progress in Human Geography*, 33(1): 74–80.

Sheehy, G. (1977) *The Silent Passage: Predictable Crises of Adult Life*, Bantam.

Sheehy, G. (1981) *Pathfinders: How to Achieve Happiness by Conquering Life's Crisis*, London: Sedgwick and Jackson.

Sherman, E. (1987) *Meaning in Mid-Life Transitions*, Albany, NY: State University of New York Press.

Simonsen, K. (2000) Editorial: The body as battlefield, *Transactions of the Institute of British Geographers*, 25(1): 7–9.

Skinner, M.W., Cloutier, D. and Andrews, G.J. (2015) Geographies of ageing: Progress and possibilities after two decades of change, *Progress in Human Geography*, 39(6): 776–799.

SkyNews (2023) Mental health services failing to consider impact of menopause, putting women at risk of suicide, 23 March, https://uk.news.yahoo.com/mental-health-services-failing-consider-151300434.html

Smith, D.M. (1994) *Geography and Social Justice*, London: Blackwell.

Soaita, A.M. and Searle, B.A. (2016) Debt amnesia: Homeowners' discourses on the financial costs and gains of homebuying, *Environment and Planning A*, 48(6): 1087–1106.

Staudinger, U.M. (1999) Social cognition and a psychological approach to an art of life, in F. Blanchard-Fields and T. Hess (eds) *Social Cognition, Adult Development and Aging* (pp 343–375), New York: Academic Press.

Staudinger, U.M. and Bluck, S. (2001) A view on midlife development from life-span theory, in M.E. Lachman (ed) *Handbook of Midlife Development* (pp 3–39), Hoboken, NJ: John Wiley and Sons, Inc.

Steffan, B. (2021) Managing menopause at work: The contradictory nature of identity talk, *Gender, Work and Organization*, 28(1): 195–214.

Stein, H.F. and Niederland, W.G. (1989) *Maps from the Mind: Readings in Psychogeography,* Norman: University of Oklahoma Press.

Stenning, A., Chan, L., Rhodes, L. and Smith, K. (2021) The everyday, in The Newcastle Social Geographies Collective (ed) *Social Geographies: An Introduction* (pp 117–122), Lanham: Rownan and Littlefield.

Stockdale, A., MacLeod, M. and Philip, L. (2013) Connected life courses: Influences on and experiences of 'midlife' in-migration to rural areas, *Population, Space and Place*, 19: 239–257.

Suomi (2023) *Vahva ja Välittävä Suomi*, Neuvottelutulos hallitusohjelmasta.

Sykes, R. (2017) Who gets to speak and why? Oversharing in contemporary North American women's writing, *Signs: Journal of Women in Culture and Society*, 43(1), 151–174.

REFERENCES

Targett, R. and Beck, V. (2022) Menopause as a well-being strategy: Organizational effectiveness, gendered ageism and racism, *Post Reproductive Health*, 28(1): 23–27.

Titma, M. (2004) Guest editor's introduction: People in post-Soviet transitional societies, *International Journal of Sociology*, 34(2): 3–10.

Torres, S. and Hunter, A. (2023) Migration and ageing: The nexus and its backdrop, in S. Torres and A. Hunter (eds) *Handbook on Migration and Ageing* (pp 1–12), Cheltenham: Edward Elgar Publishing.

Trémollieres, F.A., André, G., Letombe, B., Barthélemy, L., Pichard, A., Gelas, B. and Lopès, P. (2022) Persistent gap in menopause care 20 years after the WHI: A population-based study of menopause-related symptoms and their management, *Maturitas*, 166: 58–64.

Turek, K. and Henkens, K. (2020) How skill requirements affect the likelihood of recruitment of older workers in Poland: The indirect role of age stereotypes, *Work, Employment and Society*, 34(4): 550–570.

UK Government (2023) New scheme for cheaper hormone replacement therapy launches, Department of Health and Social Care, https://www.gov.uk/government/news/new-scheme-for-cheaper-hormone-replacement-therapy-launches

UK Parliament (2023) Menopause and the workplace: Government response to the Committee's First Report of Session 2022–2023: Fourth Special Report of Session 2022–23, https://publications.parliament.uk/pa/cm5803/cmselect/cmwomeq/1060/report.html

United Nations Department of Economic and Social Affairs (2019) *World Population Ageing 2019: Highlights*, New York: United Nations, www.un.org/en/development/desa/population/publications/pdf/ageing/WorldPopulationAgeing2019-Highlights.pdf

Verburgh, M., Verdonk, P., Appelman, Y., Brood-van Zanten, M. and Nieuwenhuijsen, K. (2020) 'I get that spirit in me': Mentally empowering workplace health promotion for female workers in low-paid jobs during menopause and midlife, *International Journal of Environmental Research and Public Health*, 17(18): 6462. doi: 10.3390/ijerph17186462

Vollset, S.E., Goren, E., Yuan, C.-W., Cao, J., Smith, A.E., Hsaio, T. … and Murray, C.J.L. (2020) Fertility, mortality, migration, and population scenarios for 195 countries and territories from 2017 to 2100: A forecasting analysis for the Global burden of disease study, *The Lancet*, 396(10258): 1285–1306.

Walker, A. (2002) A strategy for active ageing, *International Social Security Review*, 55: 121–139.

Wildman, J.M. (2020) Life-course influences on extended working: Experiences of women in a UK baby-boom birth cohort, *Work, Employment and Society*, 34(2): 211–227.

Williams, A., Lyeo, J.S., Geffros, S. and Mouriopoulos, A. (2021) The integration of sex and gender considerations in health policymaking: A scoping review, *International Journal for Equity in Health*, 20(1): 1–15.

Williams, S.J., Higgs, P. and Katz, S. (2012) Neuroculture, active ageing and the 'older brain': Problems, promises and prospects, *Sociology of Health and Illness*, 34(1): 64–78.

World Economic Forum (2020) *The Future of Jobs Report*, World Economic Forum, www3.weforum.org/docs/WEF_Future_of_Jobs_2020.pdf

Worth, N. (2009) 'Understanding youth transition as becoming: Identity, time and futurity', *Geoforum*, 40(6): 1050–1060.

Worth, N. and Hardill, I. (2015) *Researching the lifecourse. Critical Reflections from the Social Sciences*, Bristol: Policy Press.

Zimmer, M. and Hoffman, A. (2011) Privacy, context, and oversharing: Reputational challenges in a Web 2.0 world, in H. Masum and M. Tovey (eds) *The Reputation Society: How Online Opinions Are Reshaping the Offline World* (pp 175–184), Cambridge, MA: MIT Press.

Zimmerman, T. (2017) #Intersectionality: The fourth wave feminist Twitter community, *Atlantis: Critical Studies in Gender, Culture & Social Justice*, 38(1): 54–70.

Index

A

'active ageing' (Walker) 104
adulthood 10, 101
African American women 88
ageing 18, 36–37, 38–39, 89–90
ageing bias 39
ageing populations 7
ageing transitions 6
ageism 90–91, 93
agency 34–35, 55, 65
Amini, E. 3, 18, 26, 65, 78, 93
anger 27
anthropological studies 83
anxieties 44
Appadurai, A. 28
Asia 86
assumptions of stability 76
Australia 17
autobiographical bricolages 29
'autotheory' (private theory) 25
awareness activism 80

B

Baltic states 46, 49
Barnewolt, D. 55
Baruch, E. 27, 100, 102
Beauvoir, S. de 26
bioidentical products 95
biopower 24
Blackie, S. 26–27
Black midlife and menopause 19
Bluck, S. 30–31, 33, 101
body care 41
body changes 38–40
body image 39
body needs 103–104
body scale 36–37, 38, 56–57
body transitions 40–41
Boston Women's Health Collective 16, 28–29

'boundary work' 100
breastfeeding 108
Brooks-Gunn, J. 27, 100, 102
burnout 110

C

Canada 109
career peaks 9, 32, 45, 104
caring 8–9, 35–36, 47, 52–53
cessation of menses 83, 84, 85
changing jobs 51, 69–70
Channel 4 27
children 47–48, 64
chronological age 33, 85–86, 100
Ciancio de Montero, A.M. 21
class, race and ethnicity 88
codes of ethics 109
complementary medicine 42
crisis narratives 20
critical and emancipatory writing 25
critical pedagogies 27
cultural stigmatization 90–91

D

data gathering 83
Davina McCall: Sex, Myths and the Menopause (Channel 4) 27
Delanoë, D. 88
deliberate changes 52–56
DeLyser, D. 82, 107
demographic approaches 9
denationalization 59–60
destandardization hypothesis 46
developmental psychology 34
diachronicity 35
diet 41, 42–43
digital spaces 93–94
divorces 71

E

early midlife 31, 56–57
early retirement 12, 47, 49
emancipatory agency 65
emancipatory approaches to the body 39
'empty nest' trope 101
energy supplements 42
entrepreneurship 106
equality, diversity and inclusion (EDI) 109
Erikson, E. 20, 35–36
ethnicized women 27
ex-partners' living arrangements 67–68
extended families 72–75
eyesight 36

F

family ties 72–73, 76
female health 5
female hormonal ageing 85
female mortality 81
females as sicker sex 91
female writers 25
feminist archives 107–108
feminist economic approaches 57, 96
feminist ethics 8
feminist geographies 8, 82, 97, 110
financial insecurity 105–106
Finland 3–4, 11, 23
  availability of treatments 95–96
  job-seeking 69–70
  medical insurance 5, 17
  menopause 17, 77
  oestrogen products 96
Finnish Gynecological Association 17
flexible work 54, 106
Flint, M. 85
foods 41
Forstrup, M. 90
Foucauldian neoliberal techniques 24
four-day weeks 107

Frank, A.W 18–19
French Revolution 15, 81
friendships 70
future imagination 35

G

gamma-aminobutyric acid (GABA) 3–4, 5
gendered ageing 57
gendered geographies of power 97–98
gendered humour 22–24
gendered spatiality 64–65
gender equality 108
gender research in geography 99
generational consciousness 102
generativity 20, 34, 35, 37–38, 57, 62, 104
geographical attention to lifecourses 62
geographic factors 85
glasses 36
growth 49–50
Gullette, M.M. 18, 22, 24

H

Hagitude (Blackie) 26
Handbook of Midlife Development (Lachman) 30
Hanson, S. 99
health and wellbeing 42–45
healthcare policies 96
health geographies 37, 97
health supplements 3–4, 42–43, 57
heart conditions 43
'herstories' 25
historical oppression 78
hobbies 54
Hollis, J. 19, 20
home ownership 51, 59, 61–63
homes 59–76
  generativity 62
  insecurities 68–69, 75–76, 105–106
  late midlife 65–69
  and menopausing people 93

in midlife 104–105
midlife geographies 75
midlife theories 61
and youth transition 76
Hopkins, P. 7
hormone medicines 95–96, 96
'hormone replacement therapy' (HRT) 16, 79
hormone treatments 16, 79, 87, 96–97, 108, 110
see also menopause
Hormonit! (YLE) 23–24
hot flushes 40, 41, 88
housewives 55
humanistic geographies 21
humanities 10
humans as objects 21

I

I Love Dick (Kraus) 25
imagining ageing futures 35
individualism 21–22, 24
'individuation' 20
inequalities 80
Infurna, F.J. 100, 101, 105
inherited homes 65–69
institutional ethnographies 96
interdisciplinary work 83
inter-gender openness 44
intergenerational interdependencies 34
intergenerational social mobility 32
intergenerational times of silencing 86–89
intergenerational timing 47
international careers 47–48
International Women's Initiative 79
intersectional feminism 8
intersectional geographies 98
interviews 2, 11–12, 103
intra- and intergenerational relations 8, 34
introspection 19–21
Iran 89, 93

J

job losses 110
job satisfaction 54–55
Jungian psychology 19–20

K

Katz, C. 35
Kibler, E. 106
Kraus, C. 25
Krivade, A. 25–26

L

labour market volatility 106
Lachman M.E. 30
late midlife 31, 56–57
Latin America 86
Latvia 4, 11, 69–70
 generational consciousness 102
 homes in midlife 104–105
 ideation of society 63
 menopause 17, 40–41, 77
 older age and retirement 35
 post-Soviet contexts 46, 59–60
 research participants 45
 returning to 73–74
 transnational migration 51–52
Latvian Council of Science 11
laying low 50–52, 104
legitimacy of decisions 97
LGBTQIA+ 94
lifecourse literature 83
lifecourses 33, 34, 56, 66, 76, 101–102
lifecourse theories 103–104
life satisfaction 55
life transition theories 6
lived experience 2, 6, 83, 84, 102–103, 104
living below capabilities 104
Lock, M. 3
Lorde, A. 27
Loughborough University 4

M

Mahler, S.J. 97–98
maintaining health 40

Mannheim, K. 102
markers of transitions 100–101
market-driven businesses 57
market volatilities 106
Massey, D. 35
materiality of body 36–37
mature midlife 31, 56–57
McCall, D. 15, 77, 90
McCormack, M. 18, 26, 78
medical insurance 5, 17
medicalized language 82–83
medical literature 5, 85
melatonin 5
memory 89–90
'menopausal time' (Amini and McCormack) 78
menopause 5, 77–98
  class, race and ethnicity 88
  culturally contingent process 85
  and culture 83
  digital spaces 93–94
  fears 89–90
  geographic contributions 81–82
  historical oppression 78
  hot flushes 40, 41, 88
  invention of the concept 21, 81
  lived experience 84
  mainstream agendas 91
  medical term 80–82, 84
  memory 89–90
  oppressive contradictions 80
  patriarchy and ageism 81
  perceptions and cultural attitudes 87–88
  policies 108–109
  as a sickness 81, 89
  silence about symptoms 87
  social, cultural and spatial contexts 86
  statistics 83
  studies 88–89
  treatments 84–85, 91
  vasomotor symptoms 88, 92
  wellbeing strategies 93
  see also hormone treatments
menopause activism 78–79, 96, 98
menopause age 84–86
menopause awareness 15–16, 77, 78–79, 98
menopause care 87
menopause education 16
menopause exhaustion 93
menopause geographies 3, 13, 15, 82, 107
menopause jokes 24
Menopause Mandate 94, 109
menopause-related goods 97, 98
menopause research 80–81, 87–88
menopause workplace frameworks 108
menopausing 3, 15, 77–78
  crucial transformations 83
  and gender equality 107–110
  medical literature 85
  scalar processes 97
  signs of 57, 84
  supply chain strategies 94–95
  in the workplace 92–93
menstrual leave 108
menstruation 83, 84, 85, 108
mental health 44, 90
'mid-course' (Moen) 49
middle age
  anxieties 44
  defining 32–33
  derogatory talk 23
  sandwich generation 1, 34
  supplement industries 57
middle-aged women 53, 83
middle-class patriarchal relations 75
The Middle Passage (Hollis) 19
midlife 33–34
  defining 30–31, 100
  demographic approaches 9
  intergenerational relations 7
  as a process 76
  sedentary time 56
  temporality and agency 35
  theoretical research 31
midlife anxieties 24, 38
midlife body transition 107
mid-lifecourse 7, 8, 63–64

midlife crises 18, 19–21
midlife geographies 7, 99–100
midlife home 67, 75–76
midlife ideation 65
Midlife in the United States (MIDUS) 9, 32, 45
midlife migration 71–72
midlife novels 24
midlife transitions 76, 81–82, 103
migrants 46, 106
migration 9–10, 43–44, 60, 72–75
Mill, John Stuart 20
Moen, P. 49
Monk, J. 99
Moore, A. 21
multiscalar inquiries 97

N

Nap Ministry 27–28
National Health Service (NHS) 52, 110
neoliberal anxieties 22
neoliberal culture 10, 89
neoliberalism 6, 21–22, 24, 65
networks and linked lives 76
neurocultural pressures 90, 103
Newson, L. 90
nocturnal geographies 92
non-binary experience of menopause 94
non-discrimination policies 109
non-standard lifecourse transitions 32, 46
non-Western epistemologies 89
Nordic approaches 62–63
North America 86
Norway 39

O

oestrogen products 95, 96
O'Hearn, S. 109
'one size fits all' approaches 86–87
oversharing 25
overweight 38–39

P

Pain, R. 7
patriarchy 25, 27, 81, 89, 91
pensions 52, 75
perceptions of midlife 21, 31
perimenopause 3, 83, 84
'the personal self-project' (Sheehy) 20
Pessar, P.R. 97–98
physiotherapists 109
Pinkola Estés, C. 27
pleasurable work 54–55
policy makers 101
Portugal 85
postmenopause 84–85
post-socialism turbulence 102
post-Soviet Union 45–46, 59–60
post-structural feminist approaches 82
Potter, N. 15, 77, 90
'practiced intersectionality' (Lorde) 28
precarious work 70–71
pregnancy and parental leave policies 108
Premarin 86–87
presbyopia 36
private theory ('autotheory') 25
privatization 59–60
professional growth 49–50
professional learning 56
progesterone 95
psychiatry 81
psychological approaches 19, 88

Q

Queer, Black and surgical menopause-experiencing people 80
Queermenopause Collective 28

R

racialized menopause neglect 88
racism and exclusion 92–93
Radcliffe College study 102

rage 27
reconfiguring relationships 103
relationships 60, 67–76
renovating houses 66–67
reskilling 105
Rest and Resist movement 27–28
retirement planning 61
ruptured families 69–72, 74

S

Scandinavia 61–62
second-generation immigrants 43–44
The Second Sex (de Beauvoir) 26
self-esteem 38–39
self-help books 22, 24, 65
Setiya, K. 20
Shaw, W. 82, 107
Sheehy, G. 20
shift work 43
Singman de Vogelfanger, L. 21
Smellie, A. 90
social geography 85
social imagination 28
social insecurity 105
social media 94
social research 10, 82
social sciences 7
Soviet Union 45–46
soya beans 95
Spain 73
stable work 32, 55, 104
standard lifecourse transitions 31–32, 46
Staudinger, U.M. 30–31, 33, 101
Stenning, A. 107
strong ties 71–73, 74–75, 76
'successful' midlife 63
supply chains 94–95, 96

T

'tactics' of feminist action (Amini) 65
temporal boundaries 100

temporal horizons 35
tenancies 68
theorizing menopause 81, 83
'third' and 'fourth' types of old age 90
tiredness 90
Titma, M. 45–46
transformation stories 22
transitions 57–58, 101, 103–104
transnational migration 51–52, 60
transnational returns 71
Trémollieres, F.A. 87
tropes 18, 62, 101
Tunisian women 88

U

UK 11
  access to treatments 110
  agency on work schedules 55
  digital spaces 94
  discourses on menopause 16, 27, 44, 77
  hormone products 95
  improving workplaces 109
  state pensions 52
UK-based Latvian migrants 35, 37–38
uninsured and underinsured midlife 106
University College London 16
US 17, 88

V

vasomotor symptoms 88, 92
vertical ties 70

W

Walker, A. 104
washrooms 93
water 43
weak ties 70, 71–72, 73
weight gain 38–39
Western cult of youth 18
Whiteness 75

White women 88
women of colour 27
Women's Health Initiative 86, 108
Women Who Run with the Wolves (Pinkola Estés) 27
work-life changes 52–58, 105–107
workplace policies 82
workplaces 45–47, 92–94, 109
World Economic Forum 105
written language 25
'wrong' thinking 91

Y

yams 95
YLE (television channel) 23
'young family' trope 62
young midlife house ownership 61–63
youth 34, 99–102, 101
youth-obsessed societies 22
youth transition 76
'yo-yo' transitions 48, 55, 70–71

Z

Zimmer, M. 25